Praise for
The Principle of the Path

As Billy Graham's son, and a preacher myself, I have seen firsthand the devastating consequences of choosing the wrong path in life. Andy Stanley writes about the importance of following the path that is set before us as stated in the Bible. Proverbs 3:5-6: "Trust in the Lord with all your heart, and lean not on your own understanding. In all your ways acknowledge Him and He shall direct your paths." May all who read these words be obedient in their daily walk with the Savior.

> — FRANKLIN GRAHAM
> President & CEO, Billy
> Graham Evangelistic
> Association and
> Samaritan's Purse

As a young man, I did a lot of stupid things. Those dumb decisions and bad behaviors led me straight into bankruptcy and heartache. But once I changed directions and started doing smart things with my life and money, I started winning. It's really that simple. If you don't want to learn this life-changing principle like I did—the hard way—then you need to read Andy Stanley's *The Principle of the Path*. I just wish I had a copy of it twenty years ago!

When working with financially distressed families, one of the biggest challenges is getting them to see the series of bad decisions that got them into trouble in the first place. If everyone really understood—and applied—Andy Stanley's *The Principle of the Path*, I believe the whole financial landscape of America would change practically overnight.

I tell people every day, "If you keep doing what you've been doing, you'll keep getting what you've been getting."

Divorce, bankruptcy, foreclosure, failed businesses . . . these things don't happen overnight. They're the result of a consistent pattern of bad decisions. Usually all that's needed to turn someone's life around is an intentional change of direction—and that's exactly what Andy Stanley's *The Principle of the Path* is all about.

> — DAVE RAMSEY,
> host of *The Dave Ramsey
> Show* and best-selling author
> of *Total Money Makeover*

Every once in a while a book comes along that causes me to adjust the way I see myself and the world around me. This is one of those books. The subtitle pretty much says it all. This book will help you get from where you are to where you want to be! Andy Stanley's practical, biblically-grounded wisdom, self-deprecating humor, and personal example are why he is one of my favorite communicators.

— JONATHAN RECKFORD,
CEO, Habitat for Humanity
International

If you know where you want to go, this book will help you get there.

— MARK RICHT,
Head Football Coach,
University of Georgia

In what has immediately become my favorite "Andy Stanley book" (and that is saying something) the author provides proof that the choices one consciously makes today will revolutionize your life and leave a lasting impact upon the world. This book encouraged and energized me. It will allow you to see your own path with new vision.

Andy Stanley is one of three people on this planet whose words—both written and spoken—have most shaped the person I am today. While I still have miles to travel in becoming who I am supposed to be, I continue to be excited about the influence Andy has in my life and my role as a husband, a father, and communicator."

— ANDY ANDREWS,
speaker and best-selling
author of *The Traveler's Gift*

The Principle of the Path

THE PRINCIPLE OF THE PATH

How to Get from Where You Are
to Where You Want to Be

ANDY STANLEY

THOMAS NELSON
Since 1798

NASHVILLE   DALLAS   MEXICO CITY   RIO DE JANEIRO   BEIJING

Published in Nashville, Tennessee, by Thomas Nelson. Thomas Nelson is a registered trademark of Thomas Nelson, Inc.

Thomas Nelson, Inc. titles may be purchased in bulk for educational, business, fundraising, or sales promotional use. For information, please e-mail SpecialMarkets@ ThomasNelson.com.

Unless otherwise noted, Scripture quotations are taken from the HOLY BIBLE: NEW INTERNATIONAL VERSION®. © 1973, 1978, 1984 by International Bible Society. Used by permission of Zondervan Publishing House. All rights reserved.

Scripture quotations marked NASB are from the NEW AMERICAN STANDARD BIBLE®. © The Lockman Foundation 1960, 1962, 1963, 1968, 1971, 1972, 1973, 1975, 1977, 1995. Used by permission. Scripture quotations marked NKJV are from THE NEW KING JAMES VERSION. © 1982 by Thomas Nelson, Inc. Used by permission. All rights reserved. Scripture quotations marked NLT are from the *Holy Bible*, New Living Translation. © 1996. Used by permission of Tyndale House Publishers, Inc., Wheaton, Illinois 60189. All rights reserved.

Library of Congress Cataloging-in-Publication Data

Stanley, Andy.
    The principle of the path : how to get from where you are to where you want to be / Andy Stanley.
      p. cm.
   ISBN 978-0-8499-2060-8 (hardcover)
    1. Success—Religious aspects—Christianity. 2. Christian life. I. Title.
BV4598.3.S72 2008
248.4—dc22   2008050270

Printed in the United States of America

09 10 11 12 13 QW 5 4 3 2 1

TABLE
OF CONTENTS

INTRODUCTION

In the category of Top Three Dumbest Things I Ever Did is my decision to ignore an oversized Detour—Road Closed sign and drive down a stretch of I-20 between Birmingham and Atlanta before that particular section of highway was officially opened. But I was eighteen and knew everything there was to know about anything.

Well, almost everything.

I was not alone. My good friend Louie Giglio and I had some "business" in Birmingham, Alabama. Somehow we overlooked the fact that Birmingham is on Central Standard Time, and consequently, it was an hour later at home in Atlanta. I'm not sure how we overlooked that piece of trivia. We had driven to Birmingham that same afternoon and arrived at our appointment an hour early. Granted, we should have logged that detail away and planned our trip home accordingly. But we didn't.

We had promised our parents we would be back by midnight. That was after a long discussion about whether we should even go on this little jaunt across the state line. So we departed Birmingham at nine thirty, thinking we had plenty of time to make the return trip. But about twenty minutes down the road, it dawned on us that it was an hour later than we thought it was. And as fate would have it, that was about the time we arrived at the detour sign.

Back in the day, there was a twenty- or thirty-mile stretch of I-20 between Atlanta and Birmingham that for some reason the Department of Transportation just could not seem to finish. So vehicles were detoured off the interstate onto a single-lane road that meandered through a couple of small towns and a whole bunch of pasture, forests, and lowlands. The road eventually would dump back out onto the completed section of I-20, and off you would go. On our way to Birmingham that afternoon, we couldn't help but notice that the closed section of I-20 looked perfectly navigable . . . at least the section we could see. From what we could tell, all it lacked was stripes and guardrails.

So at 11:00 p.m., two hours from home with only an hour to get there, we made a really bad decision. We drove right between the words *Road* and *Closed* and headed on down the highway. Two things happened as we crossed into the great unknown. First, the notion of doing what nobody else was doing created an immediate adrenaline rush. Louie cranked up the radio, and we both rolled down our windows and began singing at the top of our lungs. I won't tell you what we were singing because that would date this story beyond recognition. There wasn't such a thing as a high five back then, so I doubt there was any actual body contact, but we were totally sure and full of ourselves in those initial moments. The second thing I noticed was that someone was following us. Fast.

My first thought was, *police*. But there weren't any blue lights. In fact, whoever it was seemed content to just follow along. That was too freaky, so I slowed down and motioned for whoever it was to pull up beside us. Turns out it was another guy from Atlanta, looking for a shortcut. We assured him that the road was completed, just not open, and off we went—side by side, lights on bright, radio blaring. Since there was no posted speed limit, we assumed there wasn't one at all. Besides, the point of a shortcut is that it is shorter. Or at least faster.

Twenty or thirty minutes later, our initial burst of enthusiasm began to wane. The farther we drove, the less sure we became. We even started slowing down. Then up ahead on the right shoulder we caught a glimpse of a black sedan. As we flew by, the headlights came on, and it pulled out onto the highway. Our stomachs dropped through the floorboards. We were sure it was the police. But once again, there were no blue lights. And the driver, whoever or whatever, was not content to follow. He was planning to pass.

Now we were really scared. At this point it would have been comforting to see blue lights. Instead, we were being chased by . . . well, we didn't know. To add to our anxiety, we were in the middle of serious nowhere. And the only things we could think about were *Walking Tall Part 2* and *The Trial of Billy Jack*. (If neither of those movie titles rings a bell, check with your father. He saw 'em.) I thought about trying to outrun the black phantom, but I knew my mom's four-door Catalina was not up to the challenge.

So we began slowing down. But our pursuer didn't. With head-lights flashing, he flew by us in a cloud of dust and gravel and almost disappeared into the darkness. As he passed, we could see that there were two people in the car, and one of them looked rather female.

That was a good sign.

But our fear suddenly changed to confusion when the driver stopped in the middle of the highway, got out of his car, and began waving his arms over his head. Clearly this guy was crazy.

Louie suggested I slow down enough to make him think we were going to stop, and then keep going. I agreed. But then we saw that the passenger in the car was, in fact, a young lady; and the driver looked to be no more than sixteen or seventeen years old. That's when it dawned on us what they were doing out in the middle of nowhere. But what we didn't know was why they inter-rupted their date to chase down a couple of strangers.

The guy in the other car rolled down his window and waved the kid over. He slid in between our two cars and blurted out, "What are you doing out here?" Actually his question was a bit more colorful than that, but that was the gist of it. And though it really wasn't any of his business what we were doing out there, it seemed like a fair question now that we knew what *he* was doing out there. But why he had chased us down remained a mystery.

Before any of us could answer, he informed us that in another mile or so the highway ended at an unfinished bridge. If we had kept going, we would have driven off the bridge into a swamp.

That would have really made us late.

Fortunately, our new friend and his girlfriend offered to lead us back to an exit ramp, and from there he told us he would show us how to get back to the county road that would eventually take us to where the completed stretch of I-20 began. We expressed our sincere gratitude, and off we went. Looking back, the decision to follow this guy over the river and through the woods was about as stupid as ignoring the Road Closed signs. For all we knew he could have been the grand dragon of a local cult. But our only other choice was to drive all the way back to where we started this misadventure. So we followed along.

True to his word, lover boy guided us through a series of back roads and state highways until we finally reached a legitimate onramp for I-20. And at around 1:30 a.m., we rolled into my driveway. I don't remember what we told our parents about why we were so late. I do know we didn't tell 'em the whole story. Some stories are better left untold.

And some roads are better left untraveled. ⌐

That's what this book is about.

ONE

Swamp My Ride

Now, if Louie and I had not been rescued by the stranger in the black Monte Carlo; and if we had, in fact, driven through the next set of barricades into a swamp, we would have done so for two reasons. And neither reason has anything to do with IQ, education, goals in life, net worth, looks, or church attendance. We would have ended up in the swamp because *that's where the road led* and *that was the road we chose.*

Anyone, regardless of race, creed, color, or sex, would have ended up in the same place had they chosen that stretch of highway. It didn't dead-end in one place for one kind of person and somewhere else for another kind. That unfinished stretch of highway was no respecter of persons. Everybody got the same treatment. And that's true of every highway, freeway, driveway, or path. It leads where it leads, regardless of who's on it.

Nothing new or original about that.

But here's where you may need some convincing. The principle you employ every time you look at a map or fire up your GPS (i.e., roads lead to the same place every time) applies to other arenas of your life as well. But what's perfectly obvious in the realm of geography is not so obvious in those other arenas. And, as we are about to discover, what's true geographically is equally true relationally, financially, physically, and academically. There is a parallel principle that affects parenting, dating, marriage, our emotions, our health, and a host of other areas as well. Just as there are physical paths that lead to predictable physical locations, there are other kinds of paths that are equally predictable.

Realizing that we are only a few pages into our time together, I don't expect you to accept my premise just yet. But before you start pushing back, consider this: What if I'm right? What if there really are financial paths that lead to predictable financial destinations? What if there are relational paths that lead to predictable relational destinations? What if there are emotional and spiritual paths that lead to specific emotional and spiritual destinations? I don't have to convince you that there are dietary paths that lead to specific health destinations. And we all know people whose lifestyle decisions led them to predictable predicaments. But what if those we-all-saw-it-coming scenarios reflect a universal law? What if there is a single unifying principle that governs what happens not only on the highway but in every area of life? I believe there is. I call it the *principle of the path*.

PRINCIPLE

I refer to this as a *principle* because this isn't a rule you follow. Truth is, the principle of the path follows you. It's not a law. You can break a law. But the principle of the path has the power to break you. It is not an idea or concept you choose to apply. As we will discover, it is being applied *to you* every moment of every day. Principles are different from rules or laws. Perhaps an example will help.

When you were in high school, you probably studied Archimedes' principle. Ring a bell? No? It ought to, because every time you get in a pool, a boat, the bathtub, or a cruise ship, you are being impacted by Mr. Archimedes' principle of buoyancy. "But wait," you argue, "that's impossible; I don't even know what it is!" Maybe not, but you are impacted just the same. And to be fair, so is everybody you know. That's the nature of a principle. You don't have to know it or apply it to be impacted by it. And that's just the beginning. The principle that explains why a drowning man sinks is the same principle that explains why the flotation device the lifeguard throws in his direction floats. Go figure.

When the principle of buoyancy is leveraged, things float. When this principle is ignored or misapplied, things sink. According to Archimedes' principle, a body immersed in liquid receives an upward thrust from the bottom toward the top, equal to the weight of the displaced liquid. So five-ounce pebbles sink, and a fifty-one-ton battleship floats. Now, Archimedes was an inventor as well as a mathematician, but he did not invent this principle—he *discovered* it. Things were sinking and floating long before he came on the scene. He simply gave the world an explanation for something that had been happening since the first duck spotted the first pond. Knowing about his principle won't keep you from sinking, but learning how to leverage it will. That's the nature of a principle.

Like Archimedes' principle, the principle of the path is not anyone's invention. It is a discovery. A discovery that explains patterns that have been observed since the beginning of time. Specifically, the principle of the path explains why many people's dreams don't come true. It explains why intelligent people with admirable goals and ambitions end up far away from where they intended to be relationally, financially, educationally, emotionally, even spiritually. It explains why people who seemingly have everything end up with nothing.

But this same principle also explains why other individuals are able to attain the life and lifestyle they have always dreamed of. As Archimedes' principle explains both why rocks sink and boats float, so this principle explains why some people do well in life while others don't. But the principle of the path is more than an explanation. Again, it is a principle, which means that once it is discovered, it can be leveraged. To leverage something is to borrow or use its power. The principle of the path is a powerful principle, and its power is available to anyone who is willing to leverage it.

What Farmers Know

If you grew up around church or on a farm, you may be familiar with the principle of the harvest. As is the case with Archimedes' principle, whether or not you are familiar with it, you've been impacted by it. The principle of the harvest states that we reap what we sow. Sow apple seeds and you will reap a harvest of apple trees. Sow watermelon seeds and you get—you guessed it—watermelons. Nothing new there. This cause-and-effect relationship is in place whether you know about it or not. And it is in place whether you agree with it or not.

Chances are you've heard the principle of the harvest applied outside the realm of agriculture. The principle of the harvest applies to friendships, finances, and marriage. What you put into something impacts what you can expect to get out of it. Neglect your marriage or your health and the outcome is predictable. You experienced this principle at work throughout your time in school. What you put in determined what you got out. This principle operated in the background of your life whether you were aware of it or not. And if someone had brought it to your attention and you refused to accept it as true, it really would not have mattered. You were going to reap what you sowed anyway. That's just how principles work. And the principle of the path is no different. But whereas I've never met anyone who disputed Archimedes' principle or the principle of the harvest, I've talked to dozens of individuals and couples who refused to accept the principle we are going to focus on in this book. And the tragedy is, believing it or not believing it doesn't change the fact that it operates in the background of our lives each and every day.

COMING UP

At the beginning of the next chapter, I'm going to introduce you to and define the principle of the path. This one powerful principle, if embraced, will empower you to identify the paths that lead to the destinations you desire in a multitude of arenas. This same principle will aid you in identifying the paths you should avoid as well. Let me be specific. If you're married, this principle will help you stay married. If you and your partner embrace this idea, your marriage will get better. If you have kids, this principle will position you to hand off your values and worldview to your children. I've seen this principle heal broken relationships. Better yet, this simple idea protects relationships from being broken to begin with. If you're single, this insight will maximize your potential for healthy and enjoyable relationships.

When applied to the realm of finance, this principle will ensure that you live with more margin and less pressure. I've seen individuals and couples take this idea to heart and within a few months dramatically change the way they handle and view their finances. Sandra and I adopted this idea early in our marriage. We've never—and I mean never—had any consumer debt of any kind. And we've never argued over money. Granted, we've only been married eighteen months but . . . Not really. We just crossed the twenty-year mark.

But that's just half of the story.

Embracing the principle of the path is the key to avoiding regret. All kinds of regret. Relational, professional, academic, moral, marital . . . as a pastor, I've heard more stories of regret than I can recount. Hundreds. I've walked with individuals and couples through bankruptcy, divorce, custody battles, lawsuits, partnerships gone bad, and kids gone wild. I've listened to count-less people tell me how badly they wish they could go back and do it all over: marry differently, date differently, spend differently, parent differently, live differently. But, of course, you can't go back. Anna Nalick is right: "Life's like an hourglass glued to the table." And for all you country music fans, Kenny Chesney is correct as well: "When your hourglass runs out of sand, you can't turn it over and start again."

Perhaps you've heard someone make the argument that experience is the best teacher. That may be true, but that's only half the truth. Experience is often a brutal teacher. Experience eats up your most valuable commodity: time. Learning from experience can eat up years. It can steal an entire stage of life. Experience can leave scars, inescapable memories, and regret. Sure, we all live and learn. But living and learning don't erase regret. And regret is more than memory. It is more than cerebral. It's emotional. Regret has the potential to create powerful emotions—emotions with the potential to drive a person right back to the behavior that created the regret to begin with. If regret can be avoided, it should be. And the principle of the path will empower you to do just that.

Now, I realize that's a big promise. I wouldn't blame you for being a bit skeptical. I'm well aware that the discount table at your local bookstore is filled to capacity with books making similar promises. But if you will indulge me for one more chapter, I think I can connect enough dots to convince you that this is not hyperbole. This is not a self-help book. I'm not offering a formula. I'm not going to provide you with seven steps. My intention is to bring to your attention a dynamic that is operating in the background of your life and the lives of the people you love. And if you accept my premise and keep reading, you will discover what

I've learned about leveraging this powerful principle for your benefit. Because like the other principles to which I've referred, the principle of the path impacts your life every single day. And like any principle, you can leverage it for your benefit or ignore it and reap a harvest of regret.

Thirty-two years ago, a stranger in a black Monte Carlo raced ahead of me on a deserted stretch of highway and saved me from driving my car into a swamp. He kept me from ending up precisely where I didn't want to be. But he did more than that. He took the time to lead me to the road that would take me where I wanted to go. My hope is that this book will do the same thing for you.

TWO

WHY BAD
THINGS HAPPEN
TO SMART PEOPLE

Once upon a time, before there were six hundred channels, DVDs, and On-Demand movies, three networks pretty much decided what Americans would and would not be allowed to watch on television. And I'm not referring to a rating system; I'm talking content. If they didn't broadcast it, there was no way to get it. During that era one of the major networks decided that it would be a good idea to broadcast *The Wizard of Oz* annually on a Sunday night. That was really significant for our family for two reasons. First, we loved *The Wizard of Oz*. Who didn't? Second, it was on Sunday night, which meant we got to stay home from church! This was an event my sister and I looked forward to almost as much as Christmas. If you were to ask my parents to recount their memories of this sacred occasion, they would be quick to point out that I watched most of the movie from behind my father's big, leather chair. The witch was a bit much for me, even in black and white. But I loved that night nonetheless.

As you probably know, the plot of this classic film revolves around Dorothy's desire to go home. After all, there's no place like home. Dorothy may have been the only adolescent to actually believe that. But this is a fairy tale, so anything is possible. Early in the film, Dorothy meets Glinda, the good witch of the east. And it is Glinda who informs Dorothy that her only option is to seek assistance from the great and powerful Oz. Unfortunately, that will require a trip to the Emerald City. Upon discovering this bit of disconcerting news, Dorothy turns to Glinda and asks, "But how do I start for the Emerald City?"

Glinda, with her head tilted to one side and her arms stretched wide to avoid crushing that impossibly large skirt, responds, "It's always best to start at the beginning—and all you do is follow the yellow brick road . . . just follow the yellow brick road." And as it turns out, Glinda was right. A bit overdressed, but she was right. Finding the Emerald City was simply a matter of following the yellow brick road. Granted, Dorothy encountered a few obstacles along the way, but she never got lost. She just kept following that yellow brick road, and eventually she found herself in the wonderful Land of Oz. Why? Because there was something special about Dorothy or her companions? No, because that's where the yellow brick road led, and that was the path she chose. Well, actually it was the path L. Frank Baum, who originally wrote the story, chose for her. But you get my point.

Wouldn't it be great if there were a yellow brick road that led to wherever it is you want to go in life? Imagine a yellow brick road that led to a marriage that made you want to come home early every day. What about a yellow brick road that led to financial security? Or a yellow brick road that led to better health? Imagine a yellow brick road that would lead you back into a relationship with someone you never thought you would be able to reconnect with—your dad, mom, son, daughter, best friend. What if there were a road that led out of the valley of guilt, shame, or even depression? If that were the case, you would stop looking for *solutions* to problems, and you would start looking for the right *path*.

Recognizing the distinction between a *solution* and a *path* is the first step in understanding the principle of the path.

Let me explain.

How absurd would it be for someone who was lost, miles away from where he wanted to be, to say, "I need a solution!"? Or to ask you to fix his problem? Wouldn't make sense, would it? When someone is where he doesn't want to be, he already knows the solution; what he needs is *direction*. There is no *fix* for being lost. To get from where we don't want to be to where we do want to be requires two things: time and a change of direction. There isn't a quick fix.

Being lost or far from where you want to be is not a problem to be solved. There is no instant solution for being lost. One gets to the place one wants to be the same way one got to the place one didn't want to be—by putting one foot in front of the other and moving in a specific direction. Cars have problems that can be fixed. Computers have problems that can be fixed. Lawn mowers have problems that can be fixed. But generally speaking, people have directions that need to be changed.

I've talked to many individuals who want to discuss their problems. But they don't really have problems. They have chosen to live in the wrong direction. They don't need a solution. They need a new direction. If you aren't sure you're buying all of this, just look back at your own life.

As you evaluate where you are relationally, professionally, financially, or even spiritually, isn't it true that when you look back, there is a pattern to your behavior? Think specifically about your finances for a moment. Isn't it true that you have followed a specific path financially that has created your current financial reality? I'm sure there are things that have happened to you financially that were beyond your control. But I'm equally sure that there is a long sequence of financial decisions you've made that explains *where you are* financially. In essence, you have followed a specific financial path, one that, if followed by others, would bring them to a similar destination. It may have been a good path that has brought you to a good place. Or you may have chosen a path that has resulted in frustration. But either way, you have followed a path. Chances are, you didn't think of it that way at the time. Like most people, you saw your financial decisions as just that: *decisions*. Individual, disconnected events. But they were not that at all. Each was actually a step in a direction. And here you are. Whether you like where you are or not.

Through the years I've talked to many individuals and couples who say they have financial problems. And they are looking for solutions—a fix. But just as there is no fix for accidentally winding up a hundred miles from where you want to be on a road trip, there is no fix when you wake up to the reality that you are far away from where you want to be financially.

Not too long ago I was being interviewed by a national organization that does Christian events for men. One of the questions they asked me went something like this: "Reverend Stanley, what would you say to the husband and father who has not done a very good job managing his finances and because of the downturn in the economy finds himself in real financial trouble? What would you suggest someone in that situation do?" I said, "I have no idea." At that point the interviewer asked the camera operator to pause for a moment. He looked at me a bit bewildered. "No idea? You don't have any advice to offer?" "No," I said. Then I went on to explain that an economic downturn doesn't so much cause problems as it reveals them. Hard times reveal where we are (and where we aren't) faster than anything else. The person who wrote the interview questions was looking for steps. A fix. A to-do list. But if a man chooses the path of financial irresponsibility, he will eventually arrive at an unenviable destination. An economic downturn just speeds up the trip.

What's true financially is also true relationally, academically, spiritually, physically, and professionally. In the rearview mirror it becomes obvious that we are all following a path of some kind. What we experience as unrelated isolated events are really steps in a specific direction. And like every physical path you've ever ventured down, this path has a specific destination.

Now, if you can't see this in your own life, I'm sure you can see it in others' lives. When you meet people who have enviable lives financially or spiritually, isn't it true that they always have stories to tell? When you start asking questions, don't you always discover that where they are is the result of a sequence of decisions that formed the path that led them to where they are? And, of course, the opposite is true as well. When you meet someone whose life is less than enviable, his story usually reveals a pattern or path as well. And at some point in his story, you think, *You should have seen that coming! You should have known where those decisions were going to take you.* In other words, he should have been able to predict his current destination based on the path he was traveling.

Looking back on our lives, the paths are evident. Looking at others' lives, the paths are evident. It is when we look ahead that we lose sight of the fact that in every arena of life, we are moving in a specific direction toward a specific destination.

Looking ahead we are often deceived into thinking that life is a series of unrelated decisions, and somehow we will end up where we want to be simply by force of will or luck. Or as I've heard so many people say, "It'll work out somehow." But if you can see a path in the rearview mirror that reflects where you've been and explains where you are, then there must be a path ahead of you as well. A path that, like all paths, has a specific and oftentimes predictable destination.

And that brings us, at last, to the principle of the path. Here it is:

Direction—not intention—determines our destination.

The direction you are currently traveling—relationally, financially, spiritually, and the list goes on and on—will determine where you end up in each of those respective arenas. This is true regardless of your goals, your dreams, your wishes, or your wants. The principle of the path trumps all those things. Your current direction will determine your destination. And like every principle, you can leverage this one to your advantage or ignore it to your disadvantage. Just as there are paths that have led us *to* places we never intended to be, there are paths that lead us *away* from those places as well.

Whereas no one disputes the validity of this principle as it relates to planes, trains, and automobiles, the conflict starts when it is applied to the other areas we have touched on. But as we dig deeper, I think you will begin to see that the principle of the path governs all aspects of life; including dating, marriage, child-raising, career, finances, health—you name it. Direction—not intentions, hopes, dreams, prayers, beliefs, intellect, or education—determines destination. I know it's tempting to believe that our good intentions, aspirations, and dreams somehow have the ability to do an end run around the decisions that we make on a daily basis. But at the end of the day, the principle of the path determines the outcome. Simply put, you and I will win or lose in life by the paths we choose.

As I'm writing this chapter, our country has been rocked once again by a sexual scandal involving a high-profile national leader. By all accounts, this is a smarter-than-average man. He completed his undergraduate studies at Princeton University and then headed to Harvard University, where he earned his juris doctor degree to practice law. His rise to prominence began in the

Manhattan district attorney's office, where he successfully nailed the infamous Gambino organized crime family.

Years later, he served as a state attorney general. In that capacity, he acted as an outspoken crusader who boldly tackled white-collar crime, securities fraud, mutual fund scandals, and price fixing. At age forty-seven, he was elected governor of one of our nation's most influential states. He was a young man at the top of his game. That is, until March 2008, when the *New York Times* uncovered a dark truth about the governor: this outspoken critic of corruption frequently hired prostitutes. Within days, he fell from his lofty political perch to become the laughingstock of Letterman and Leno on late-night TV.

But how? *How did a guy with such a promising career suddenly fall?*

Actually, there was nothing sudden about his undoing. His fall was inevitable. The end of this story was determined years ago when he chose a path that, from the very beginning, had dishonor, disgrace, and dismissal as the destination. Direction determines destination. Every time.

Generally speaking, we don't abandon the clearly marked paths because we are looking for trouble. There's always something about the alternate routes that is powerfully appealing. They promise shortcuts of more direct and oftentimes pleasurable routes to wherever it is we are trying to go. It is easy to become enamored of the siren call of the wrong path and ignore the fact that we're heading away from our values, goals, dreams, or commitments. Think about the times you've allowed a powerful emotional appeal to turn your head, grab your attention, and take you off task.

- Zero percent financing and no money down . . .
- She makes me feel like I used to feel . . .
- But he's rich . . .
- That's how business is done here . . .
- No payments for twelve months . . .

Perhaps you are already beginning to identify paths you've chosen in the past that led you to places you did not want to go—relational patterns you were committed to avoiding; financial habits that have left you with pressures you never anticipated; an ethical compromise that promised a reward but left you with consequences you never imagined would be part of *your* story. And perhaps you can think back to the day you stepped onto the path that has led to regret. If so, you are already beginning to see how the principle of the path has been at work in your life. You don't have problems to fix; you have directions that need to change. It is time to begin living in the right direction. For just as this powerful principle explains how you've arrived where you are, it offers hope for the future as well. And, like every principle, once you understand how it works, you can leverage it to your advantage.

As I mentioned earlier, I didn't invent this principle. It has been in operation since the beginning of time. But unlike Archimedes and his principle of buoyancy, I can't take credit for discovering it either. One of—if not *the*—earliest explanations and applications of this principle is found in the ancient writings of King Solomon. In the next chapter we will take a look at how one of the wisest men who ever lived illustrates this extraordinary principle.

THREE

THE GREAT DISCONNECT

I'm a reasonably smart person. College took me a year longer than most people, but I finally graduated with a three-point-something. However, when it comes to following directions, I'm definitely *not* smarter than a fifth grader. I get lost easily and often. My wife would attest to the fact that I've pretty much mastered the "art of lostness." It is so bad that when Sandra sends me on an errand, she carries her phone around the house with her, because she knows I'm going to call. This is in spite of the fact that she sends me out with a map with the route highlighted in yellow, along with a complete set of written directions. My intentions are good. I'm just lousy with directions. And she knows it. The kids know it. Heck, everybody who knows me knows it. I mean well. But my good intentions don't really make any difference. I still get turned around.

The upside to all of this is that I can speak as an authority on the art of getting and being lost. There are three things you should know about those of us who are directionally challenged. First, we don't get lost on purpose. Nobody does that. In fact, just the opposite is true. Since we know we are likely to get lost, we work hard at paying attention and following directions. But we just don't do well in unfamiliar territory.

The second thing I've learned about getting lost is that I never know exactly when it happens. I never know when I've crossed that line between *I know exactly where I am* and *I have no idea where I am.* I never know the precise moment in which I've made an incorrect turn or taken a wrong route. There is never a moment when a light goes off in my brain and I think, *Gee, I just got lost. If I back up a hundred feet, I'll be un-lost.* Being lost is something that dawns on me. Usually after I've been lost for . . . well, I don't know how long I'm lost before I realize I'm lost. Which I guess is the point I'm trying to make.

There's a third thing about getting lost. The road I'm on always determines where I end up. Pretty insightful, eh? It really doesn't matter where I *intended* to be; the path I take determines my ultimate destination. Plans, intentions, spousal expectations . . . none of that counts. I always end up where the road I've chosen takes me. And that, as you know by now, is the theme of this book.

From Where I Sit

My observation (and experience, for that matter) indicates that humans have a propensity for choosing paths that do not lead in the direction they want to go. For much of our decision making, we lean hard into our intentions and pay very little attention to the direction of the path we've chosen. I see it all the time. Even with very smart people.

It breaks my heart how many people I speak with who don't connect the dots between the choices they make and the outcomes they experience. They've come to believe the popular notion that as long as their intentions are good, as long as their hearts are in the right place (whatever that means), as long as they do their best and try their hardest, it doesn't really matter which path they take. They believe somehow they will end up in a good place.

But life doesn't work that way.

There is an amazing piece of literature tucked away in the book of Proverbs that illustrates this disconnect better than anything else I know of. In Proverbs 7, Solomon described an encounter that he witnessed from the vantage point of his upstairs window. Because he was physically removed from what he saw, he could not hear what the characters were saying to each other. But he provided us with their conversation as he imagined it. It's also possible that this account is a parable based upon his personal experience. Whether autobiographical or an observation, his story provides extraordinary insight into our tendency to disconnect direction from destination.

Solomon wrote:

At the window of my house I looked out through the lattice. I saw among the simple, I noticed among the young men, a youth who lacked judgment. (Prov. 7:6–7)

Solomon looked out his window and saw a kid. We don't know how old this kid was, but from what we learn later, we know he was at least north of puberty. Solomon described this kid as "simple" and lacking "judgment." We may be tempted to ask, "How did he know?" And the answer is, all youths lack judgment. They are all "simple" or naive. All youths lack judgment, because judgment requires time and experience. Young people haven't lived long enough to acquire the experience that *can* produce good judgment. I say *can* because experience doesn't always lead to good judgment. But experience is certainly critical to good judgment.

Shaunti Feldhahn, in her fascinating book *For Parents Only*, cites a study claiming that the frontal lobe of the human brain doesn't fully develop until the midtwenties. The frontal lobe is where our reasoning skills reside. This explains why adolescents often engage in high-risk activities—they don't make the connection between their choices and the potential consequences. The point is that all youths lack the judgment that *can* come with age and experience. This seemingly insignificant detail is actually important to the narrative, as you are about to discover.

> He was going down the street near her corner, walking along in the direction of her house at twilight, as the day was fading, as the dark of night set in. (vv. 8–9)

Now, you don't have to be a Bible scholar to anticipate where this story is heading, do you? A young guy cruising the streets at sunset, heading in the direction of a specific woman's home. As we will see in a second, he knew who this woman was, and he knew she was married. And apparently he knew that her husband was out of town and that she would be prowling around the street corner, looking for . . . well, just looking. That alone should have stopped him in his tracks. But it didn't. In fact, that was the very reason he was headed in her direction.

If we were able to get inside this kid's head and tap into the soundtrack he had chosen for this particular evening's activities, we might have heard "Party Like a Rock Star" or, if he was a fan of classic rock, perhaps, "Born to Be Wild." Either way, he was confident that this was going to be a night to remember—and perhaps one to brag to his friends about the next day during PE.

Meanwhile, back at the window, Solomon was watching this young man, and there was a soundtrack playing in his head as well. The music from *Jaws*. Why? Because there was a marked contrast between what this kid was expecting to experience and what Solomon knew was in his future. Why? Because the older, wiser king understood from experience where this path would lead. The adolescent was preoccupied with what he believed would be an exciting event—a night of passion. A night disconnected from every other event in his life. But Solomon knew better. This night was not an isolated event disconnected from all the other events in this young man's life. This night was a step down a path. A path, like all paths, that leads somewhere. This particular path had a predictable destination. But you don't need to be the wisest man in the world to know that. You could predict the outcome of this encounter with nothing to draw on but your own experience or the experience of someone you know. Funny how that works. What's so obvious to those watching often escapes us.

The story continues:

Then out came a woman to meet him, dressed like a prostitute and with crafty intent. (She is loud and defiant, her feet never stay at home; now in the street, now in the squares, at every corner she lurks.) (vv. 10–12)

Solomon knew a thing or two about women. He made his share of poor choices in this arena. He knew from experience that this woman was toxic. And having been there himself, he also understood why this young man couldn't see it.

She took hold of him and kissed him and with a brazen face she said: "I have fellowship offerings at home; today I fulfilled my vows. So I came out to meet you; I looked for you and have found you!" (vv. 13–15)

This section requires a bit of explanation. When this woman said she had fellowship offerings at home, she was essentially saying, "Look, I'm not a hooker. I have plenty of money at home. I'm not after your money—I want you!" She was also implying that she had been to the temple and had everything squared away with God. Having taken her sin bucket and dumped it out at the altar, she was ready to fill it up again . . . with him!

As extreme as that sounds, her version of religion is not too far removed from our approach. If you're like some of my Catholic friends, you go to confession, dump out all of your sin in a confessional booth, get absolved, and then the next week you feel free to pick up where you left off. We Protestants do the same thing, but with one difference: we skip the confessional booth. Instead, we go right to the source. We pray something along the lines of, "Dear heavenly Father, please forgive me of all of my sins." We're taught that at that point, he takes out his big eraser and cleans our sin slates. Like the woman in the story, we are quick to ask for forgiveness but slow to actually repent and walk away from our sin. Granted, that whole approach is absurd when you think about it. And it is certainly an insult to God, but it works for us. We get both the relief that comes with forgiveness and the thrill that comes with sin.

Of course, this young man wasn't thinking about the absurdity of her religious system. He was thinking, *If my friends could see me now.* At that point he pumped up the volume of his soundtrack to a ten and pinched himself to be sure this wasn't a dream. Even if Solomon was to call down from the window to warn him, the kid wouldn't have heard him over the seductive words he heard next:

"I have covered my bed with colored linens from Egypt. I have perfumed my bed with myrrh, aloes and cinnamon. Come, let's drink deep of love till morning; let's enjoy ourselves with love!" (vv. 16–18)

And just in case he was wondering, she added:

"My husband is not at home; he has gone on a long journey. He took his purse filled with money and will not be home till full moon." (vv. 19–20)

Well, that pretty much clinched it right there. Not only did he not have to worry about her husband catching them but he could hang around for breakfast. Watch a little TV. Heck, he could spend the entire weekend. This just kept getting better. From his perspective, that is. But Solomon saw this situation in an entirely different light. Listen to his take.

> With persuasive words she led him astray; she seduced him with her smooth talk. All at once he followed her like an ox going to the slaughter. (vv. 21–22)

What? An ox heading *where*? Wait a minute, Solomon. Don't you mean "like a celebrity into a club?" An ox to the slaughter? It certainly doesn't look that way to the casual observer. And it certainly didn't look that way to our young friend. But Solomon was not finished with his creative use of language. He had two more animal analogies for emphasis.

> ... like a deer stepping into a noose till an arrow pierces his liver, like a bird darting into a snare, little knowing it will cost him his life. (vv. 22–23)

In case you didn't get the ox to the slaughter, how 'bout a deer stepping into a noose, with a bloodied arrow hanging from its bowels? Still don't get the picture? How about this: this kid was like a clueless bird caught in a snare. Solomon's point, as if he hadn't made it abundantly clear, was that this young man was throwing away his future. Possibly his life. Of course, were the young man able to read Solomon's mind, he would have shouted back, "You're sounding a lot like my dad! Besides, what does an old man know about love and passion anyway? This isn't just a date. It's a once-in-a-lifetime event. I'm not an ox, a deer, or a bird. Mind your own business."

At this point in Solomon's narrative, he turned a corner and addressed his broader audience. These next words are directed to you and me.

Now then, my sons, listen to me; pay attention to what I say. Do not let your heart turn to her ways or stray into her paths. (vv. 24–25)

There's our word. *Paths.* This was a path, not an event. Pay attention to this next observation:

Many are the victims she has brought down; her slain are a mighty throng. (v. 26)

Many. Solomon debunked the notion that there was anything unique about what this kid was experiencing. It may have been unique for him. But this experience represents a well-worn path: a path that leads to death in spite of what the naive kid may have wanted to argue. If Solomon could have called a time-out in the story and gotten this kid's undivided attention, he might have said something along the lines of, "Listen, buddy. I hate to break it to you, but there's nothing unique or special or rare about this. You may have never 'felt this way before,' but a lot of other people have. And if they were here to tell you their stories, you would think twice. You're part of a crowd. A herd. A flock. There is nothing new here. And the outcome is all too predictable. She's done more than capture your imagination. She's writing a script for your future. You are a dead man walking!"

Driving home the point, Solomon added:

Her house is a highway to the grave, leading down to the chambers of death. (v. 27)

A highway? Yep. A four-lane interstate with an HOV lane. Again, there's nothing new about this. Nothing unique. Just another young man who has chosen a path that will take him precisely to where he doesn't want or plan to be. There was a disconnect. The disconnect in Solomon's scenario is easy to see, at least for us. A young man who wanted his life to be relationally richer chose a path that would ultimately undermine his relationships. A young man who yearned for something good chose a path that led to something not good. A youth striving to prove his independence chose a well-worn path that had the potential to strip him of his independence. There was a disconnect. Solomon saw it from his window. I've seen similar disconnects from my imaginary window as well. And so have you.

Nothing New

We all have a propensity for choosing paths that do not lead in the direction we want to go. In a later chapter I will give you my take on what causes this apparent lapse in reason. But for now I want to focus on how this dynamic plays itself out in our world. Perhaps in your world. For example:

- A single woman says, "I want to meet and one day marry a great Christian guy who's really got his act together" . . . but then she dates whoever asks her out, as long as he's cute.

- A single guy says, "I want a great sex life once I'm married" . . . but he "practices" with every girl he dates along the way.

- A married woman says, "I want to have a great relationship with my husband" . . . but she makes the children a priority over him.

- A husband says, "I want my kids to respect me as they grow up" . . . and then he openly flirts with other women in the neighborhood.

- A young Christian says, "I want to develop a deep and lasting intimacy with God" . . . so he gets up every morning early and reads the newspaper.

- A man says, "I want to grow old and invest the latter years of my life in my grandchildren" . . . but then he neglects his health.

- A couple says, "We'd like our children to develop a personal relationship with God and choose friends who have done the same" . . . but then they skip church every weekend and head to the lake.

- Newlyweds determine to be financially secure by the time they reach their parents' age . . . then adopt a lifestyle sustained by debt and leveraged assets.

- A high school freshman intends to graduate with a GPA that will afford him options as he selects a college . . . but neglects his studies.

Obviously, the list could go on and on. And the people my list represents have legitimate goals *and* oftentimes every good intention of reaching them. But like the naive young man in Solomon's story, the paths they choose eventually bring them to a destination that is entirely different from the one they intended. And this isn't rocket science. We shouldn't need someone to connect these dots for us. If your goal is to drop two dress sizes, you don't eat lunch at a donut shop. If you desire to remain faithful to your spouse, you don't linger in an online chat room with members of the opposite sex. Those aren't pastimes. Those are pathways. They lead somewhere.

One Wednesday, late in the afternoon, I heard a tap on my office door. I was at my desk, working on my weekend talk. Looking up, I saw a friend of mine who does not attend our church appear with a somewhat troubled look on his face. I was surprised to see him. I didn't know that he even knew where my office was. But there he stood. I invited him in to take a seat. For the next thirty minutes he shared with me, in painful detail, about his financial woes. He was in a hole that was getting deeper by the week.

I'm no financial planner, but the whole time my friend was talking, I was thinking, *You should have seen this coming. And what you couldn't see coming you should have been prepared for.* For years they had been living beyond their means. Simply put, spending more than they were making, which, by the way, is a path. It is not just a financial decision. It leads somewhere. And in my friend's case, he had reached the destination . . . and was shocked!

Everything was fine until his company hit a rough spot and decided there would be no year-end bonuses. Problem was, my buddy had already spent his. On top of that, he had maxed out a home equity line of credit and had one leased car and one conventional car loan, along with other miscellaneous debt. He was in serious trouble.

Fighting back his emotion, he confessed he didn't understand how all this had happened. Then he played the God card. "Andy, why would God let this happen? I've always done my best to provide for my family." Talk about a disconnect. So now God was responsible? Like many people, he desired one thing—financial security—but headed down a path that would lead him to a very different destination.

THAT PAINFUL LOOK

As I have said throughout our time together, it is much easier to see these dynamics at work in other people than it is in ourselves. As you read through my list a few paragraphs back, no doubt specific faces and names came to mind. You might have even thought, *So-and-so needs to read this.* And you may be right. But before you start putting initials beside specific paragraphs in this book, perhaps you should pause and do a bit of self-examination:

- Are there disconnects in your life?
- Are there discrepancies between what you desire in your heart and what you are doing with your life?
- Is there alignment between your intentions and your direction?

Not too long ago, I had a Solomon moment of my own. What I am about to describe happened over the course of about thirty seconds, but it will take you longer than that to read. I was sitting in traffic about fifty yards from a traffic light at a large intersection close to where I live. There were four lanes. Two lanes went straight at the light. The two lanes to my left were left-turn lanes. All four lanes were waiting for the light to change. When the left turn signal turned green, the two lanes to my left started moving while the other two lanes, including the one I was in, waited for a green light. To my right I saw two teenage girls come running down a slight embankment. They were two cars in front of me, still a long way from the intersection where they should have gone to cross the street. They were laughing and talking. They paused long enough to look left and right; then they darted out between the cars in the two lanes that were still waiting for the light. That's when I had my Solomon moment.

I saw their future.

They assumed all four lanes were stopped and waiting for the light to change. What they failed to notice was that two of the lanes were full of moving cars, which by this time were really moving as they raced to make it through the green arrow. If I could have frozen time, gotten out of my car, and asked these two precious young ladies why they didn't walk up to the intersection, push the pedestrian crosswalk button, and wait for the little white Walk sign to illuminate, I'm sure they would have had a good explanation. This way was shorter. They were in a hurry. Who was I to interfere in their business? I don't know how they might have responded. Their decision to cross four lanes of traffic made perfect sense to them. But they didn't see what I saw. And as they ran between the cars in front of me, laughing the entire time, they never saw the green Dodge Ram pickup truck that slammed into their torsos and launched their bodies through the air. It is the most horrible thing I've ever witnessed. And I knew it was going to happen, before it happened.

My 9-1-1 call was the first one the operator received. Traffic stopped. People jumped out of their cars. Both girls were on the pavement and not moving. I was convinced they were dead. Fortunately, a nurse was one of the first people on the scene. The police arrived moments later. And I drove home very shaken up. The next day I went to the police station to see if I could get any information on the girls or the driver. I was unsuccessful. For the next two days I called everybody I knew who might be able to connect me with either the family of the girls or the gentleman who hit them. Eventually I found out that both girls survived with minor injuries, which I still can hardly believe. There were so many eyewitnesses that the driver was not charged. But I have to believe he replays that scene over and over in his mind.

In a dramatic, maybe overly dramatic way, my experience at the intersection that afternoon underscores the message of this chapter as well as this entire book. I don't know where those two young ladies were *intending* to go, but I'm confident they were not intending to run out in front of a moving truck. And I'm confident that North Fulton Hospital was not on their list either. But intentions are of little consequence. Direction is everything. Direction determines destination. This is why we cannot afford to live disconnected lives. When we discover those subtle and some-times not-so-subtle discrepancies between intent and lifestyle, we should stop and pay attention. We should break the habit of drawing a circle around individual decisions and events and dis-missing them as isolated occurrences. These are steps. Steps that lead somewhere. Because life is connected.

BACKING UP

If you've ever gotten lost while driving (and who hasn't?), you know that if you backtrack far enough, you can usually get your bearings and be on your way. Worst case, you've wasted a few min-utes or hours. But when you get lost in life, you can't backtrack. When you get lost in life, you don't waste minutes or hours. You can waste an entire season of your life. Choosing the wrong path in life will cost you precious years. Nobody wants to do that. Nobody wants to wake up in his fifties and wish he had taken a different path in his thirties. Nobody wants to arrive at the end of a marriage and wish she had taken a different path during her dat-ing years. Think about it. You only get to be twenty once. You get one senior year. You get one first marriage. The path we choose at those critical junctions doesn't just determine our destination the following year, but for the following season of life.

So once again:

- Are there disconnects in your life?
- Are there discrepancies between what you desire in your heart and what you are doing with your life?
- Is there alignment between your intentions and your direction?

The principle of the path is operating in your life every minute of every day. You are currently on a financial path of some kind. You are on a relational path. You are continuing down a moral and ethical path. And each of these paths has a destination. My hope is that by becoming aware of this powerful principle, you will have the wisdom to know which path to choose and the courage to stay the course.

FOUR

SHOULD'VE SEEN THAT COMING

In his song "Letter to Me," Brad Paisley reflects on what he would put in a letter if he had the opportunity to send one back in time to himself at age seventeen. That's a pretty fascinating thought. Based on what you know now, what would you say if you could go back and tell yourself something at seventeen? The problem, of course, is that we would tell ourselves pretty much the same stuff our parents told us. And since we didn't listen to them, chances are we wouldn't listen to ourselves. Brad alludes to that when he writes:

> *Each and every time you have a fight*
> *Just assume you're wrong and dad is right*

I know this is a bit absurd to think about, but let's think about it anyway for a moment. What would you tell yourself at seventeen, and what difference might it have made if you had actually taken your own advice? Imagine being able to warn yourself at seventeen about something or someone that would cross your path at twenty-one. Imagine the investment advice you could give yourself!

Life would be so much easier the second time around if we had an opportunity to learn from our first time around. But we don't. Primarily because we only go around once. So we are left to make decisions without the benefit of the experience necessary to make informed decisions. Or, as we argued in the last chapter, we are left to choose paths with no clear knowledge of where they lead. How do you know which way to go when you've never been where you are going?

Take marriage, for example. Single people shouldn't have to choose a marriage partner. What do they know about marriage? It's a bit absurd if you think about it. Choosing a life partner should be reserved for people who know what they are doing. Choosing a marriage partner should be reserved for people who know something about marriage.

I know. Then how would anyone get married in the first place? But you see my point. There are many life destinations we've never visited but desire with all our hearts to see and experience. And our only option is to pick a path and hope it will get us there. But how do you know? Besides, in addition to life being a series of decisions, life is a series of firsts. First date, first kiss, first semester away from home, first job, first marriage, first kid, first investment decision, first house, first loan . . . And every one of those firsts is a first step in a direction. Every first is a first step down a path. How the heck are we supposed to know where those things go? It is our first!

That's what these next few chapters are about: choosing specific paths with specific destinations in mind.

EYES ON THE ROAD

The idea of making life decisions in arenas where we lack life experience should put a little fear in all our hearts. But I don't run into too many people paralyzed by indecision. Instead of carefully analyzing the destinations associated with the various path options offered, our tendency is to charge down the path of least resistance, oblivious to the obvious.

Let me explain.

As I mentioned in the first chapter, I've talked to far too many people who are trying desperately to backtrack down paths they wish they had never taken, usually in the financial or relational arenas. Some have acquired too much debt or are in bad marriages. Others are entangled in business with people they wish they'd never met.

I imagine you've had a few of those conversations yourself. And isn't it true that—as they tell you about how their marriages are upside-down, their finances are a wreck, they made the perfectly wrong career choice, they moved in with someone when they should have moved out—as they tell their stories, you are dying to ask, "Didn't you see this coming? Wasn't there anything along the way that gave you a heads-up as to where this was going to take you? Weren't you even suspicious? Surely there were some early warning signs. Something?"

Well, while you may sit through those kinds of conversations *wanting* to ask those questions, I usually come right out and ask. That's partly a pastor thing and partly a curiosity thing. And guess what? Nine out of ten times there were some red flags, some hesitation, some early warning signs. Often they'll admit someone *did* try to get their attention with a word of caution, but they ignored the advice. They figured everything would somehow work out. Which, of course, is true. Everything *somehow* works out. Every decision has an outcome, and every path has a destination. And so there they are, exactly where they don't want to be—but exactly where their paths led them. And now life is complicated. Unnecessarily complicated. Unnecessarily, because the warning signs were all in place. Again, they were oblivious to the obvious.

But it doesn't have to be that way.

OPTIONS

About twenty years ago, I bumped into a verse in the book of Proverbs that has empowered me and my family to avoid countless complications. The unnecessary kind. In fact, this verse inspired Sandra and me to pray a prayer that we still recite to this day. Actually, recite is a bit weak. This is a prayer we cling to. I've included the prayer at the end of this chapter. But first, let's take a look at the verse that inspired it:

The prudent see danger and take refuge, but the simple keep going and suffer for it. (Prov. 27:12)

This verse introduces us to two kinds of people—the prudent and the simple. Elsewhere in Proverbs these fellow travelers are referred to as *wise* and *naive*. Both are headed down the same path. Both "see danger," but they react differently. And, consequently, they experience two very different outcomes.

Life-changing, huh? Okay, maybe not. At least not on the surface. So follow me for a moment as we take a deeper look. Let's start with the first half:

"The prudent see danger and take refuge . . ."

In the book of Proverbs, the term *prudent* is used interchangeably with *wise*. So a prudent person is a wise person. The implication here is that a prudent man or woman understands that all of life is *connected*. He is aware of the cause-and-effect relationship between what he chooses today and what he experiences tomorrow, what he chooses during one season of life and his experience in a future season—for better or worse. Consequently, prudent people look as far down the road as possible when making decisions. Every decision. After all, they understand that today and tomorrow are *connected*. As the author of Proverbs states, they stay on the lookout for signs of trouble up ahead. Today's decisions are informed and influenced by their impact on tomorrow. Drawing on their own experience or the experience of others, they anticipate the future and choose accordingly. They ask what I often refer to as *the best question ever*: "In light of my past experience, and my future hopes and dreams, what's the wise thing to do?" The prudent draw upon the wealth of data that life has already provided them and then take appropriate action when they see danger ahead.

PART TWO

In the second half of the verse, we are introduced to a second category of folks: the simple.

". . . but the simple keep going and suffer for it." (v. 12)

Simple is used interchangeably with the term *naive*. In contrast to the prudent, the simple or naive person lives as though life is *dis*connected; as if there is no connection between today's choices and tomorrow's experiences. When the simple "see danger," they don't take evasive action. They keep going.

Notice, I said they *live* as if life is disconnected. They don't necessarily believe that to be the case. If you were to ask them, "Do you think there is a connection between the choices you make today and what you will experience in the future?" they would in all likelihood answer yes. Again, it is not that they don't *believe* life is connected. The point is they don't live as if it is.

"Who would be so . . . naive?" you ask. Pretty much everybody at some point. Every time you eat something you know you will regret, you fall into this category. Every time you talk yourself out of exercising, you talk yourself out of a preferred future. Every time you light up a cigarette, lie to your spouse, or spend money you don't have, you *act* as if today is in no way connected to tomorrow. You "see danger." Yet instead of "taking refuge," you "keep going." You know life is connected. You just don't live as if it is. You make decisions today as if today is isolated from tomorrow.

We've all heard that experience is the best teacher. But the truth is, about the only thing most of us learn from experience is what to expect when we repeat the same bad decisions. We've all said, "I'll never do that again" about something. We knew what the outcome would be, but we kept going anyway.

Course Correction

The primary difference between the prudent and the simple is not what they see but how they respond to what they see. The prudent *see* danger and take refuge. The simple *see* danger and keep going. The prudent see danger and change their course. They act on what they see. The simple simply do not. The prudent act as if *then* is *now*; as if the *future* is the *present*. The simple respond as though tomorrow will always be tomorrow. The prudent respond now.

When the prudent identify behaviors turning into habits, they do something while they can. The simple keep going. When the prudent sense a relationship moving in an unhealthy direction, they do something. The simple keep going. When the prudent see trouble on their financial horizon, they do something. The simple keep spending. After all, didn't Jesus tell us not to worry about tomorrow?

THE FINAL ANALYSIS

The proverb closes with a very specific prediction. Actually, it is more like a promise or a warning.

". . . the simple keep going and suffer for it." (v. 12)

Suffer "for" what? For being oblivious to the obvious. The simple suffer for refusing to act on what they see. They suffer because they live as if there is no connection between the choices of today and the experiences of tomorrow. They overlook the fact that every path has a destination.

This is a truth many people have a difficult time accepting—for themselves, anyway. But like it or not, decisions have consequences. For some behaviors, there is a point of no return. There is a point at which it becomes impossible to sidestep consequences.

When it dawns on us that the undesirable but ever-so-predictable outcome of our choices is bearing down on us, we move into victim mode. Christians start talking about forgiveness as if somehow forgiveness serves as an escape hatch from the outcome of bad decisions. This is when people threaten to sue or countersue. Suddenly we want a second chance. We begin talking about turning over a new leaf. This is when the formerly religious start showing up in church. We are quick to remind the world that nobody is perfect. And if all else fails, we play the fairness card: *it's not fair that this is happening to me!*

When *we* are the ones facing the inevitable consequences of our decisions, it really doesn't seem fair. But when it's someone else arriving at the destination his path led him to, all his attempts to avoid the inevitable strike us as a bit amusing. After all, what did he expect? Actually, I know what he expected. He expected to be the exception to the rule, an exception to the principle of the path.

When the inevitable becomes the unavoidable, it is not unusual for us to start pointing our fingers at God. The same God who inspired a king several thousand years ago to pen the very warning we carelessly ignored. The same God who preserved this warning for us over the course of history so that it would be available to us in multiple languages, versions, covers, and colors. I really don't think God is to blame.

You've heard it. Perhaps you've said it: "How could God let this happen to me? I'm a good person. I've gone to church. Where's the love? Where's the forgiveness?" Well, the love is reflected in the warning. You warn people you love. And experiencing the outcomes of our decisions has nothing to do with forgiveness. If you don't believe me, think about how your algebra teacher would have responded if you had dropped to your knees at her desk and begged for forgiveness after flunking an exam you didn't study for. To avoid an awkward moment, she may have extended her hand and pronounced you forgiven. But that wouldn't change your grade. It may help your relationship, but not your GPA. Forgiveness and consequences are two different things. One does not override the other.

Here's why.

God often works through principles. Principles make life somewhat predictable. The cause-and-effect nature of principles creates the potential for predictable outcomes. Without principles, life would be completely random. Principles are what enable us to plan with some element of confidence. Just as you dare not ignore the principle of gravity, you would be wise not to ignore the principle of the path. At the end of the day, direction, not intention, determines destination. You can't pray your way out of that. You can't talk your way out of that. And you can't repent your way out of that. It is the way God designed the world to work.

As I write these words, I have a dear friend whose lung cancer just raised its ugly head for the second time. He was told that if it ever returned, it would probably be fatal. Our hearts are broken. But no one is totally shocked. He's smoked since he was a teenager. Does that make it any less painful? Nope. Do I still pray for him? Yep. Does God still care? Absolutely. Will forgiveness reverse this? No. Will his teenage son learn something through this? I hope so. Does everybody who smokes die of lung cancer? No. Is God punishing him? I don't believe so. He chose a path. He chose it because most of the people around him chose it as well. His intention was not to leave his son fatherless or his wife a widow. But direction trumps intention every time. Years ago he saw "danger" but didn't take refuge. He kept going. And now he and the people he loves the most are suffering for it.

The principle of the path, like all principles, is universal. It is not a respecter of men. It doesn't matter whether you're rich or poor, young or old, famous or unknown—nobody is immune to this principle. In some ways, it levels the playing field.

Speaking of playing fields, since I live in the city of Atlanta, the Michael Vick saga sure hit close to home. Literally. I'm not an

NFL junkie, but watching Mike play football was like watching art in motion. At times he appeared beyond human—arguably the finest running quarterback in NFL history. Here was a guy whose performance on the football field revitalized the Atlanta Falcon franchise. At just twenty-four, Vick was offered a ten-year, $137 million contract. Virtually overnight the entire world became his stage. His performances inspired budding athletes from every field to dream big.

Who would have guessed that a man with so much raw talent, unique ability, and remarkable opportunity would find himself sitting in a federal prison? I wrestled with whether or not to even refer to his story in this book. I always avoid piling on and I never mention famous people in a negative light when I'm speaking. But since Vick's story is so public and since he has come out and acknowledged his poor choices, it didn't seem off-limits.

My point in mentioning it at all is this: if someone with that much talent, that much potential, that many connections, and that much money could not avoid arriving at the destination to which his path of choice led him, what makes you and me think we can? The writer of Proverbs would answer that question with one word: naïveté.

I know what you might be thinking. *Well, I know this guy who blah-blah-blah, and nothing bad happened to him! He didn't arrive at a bad destination.* To which I would add, "Yet." But there are exceptions. My wife's grandmother smoked for forty years and celebrated her ninety-seventh birthday last month! But I'm not telling my kids that smoking is the key to a long and happy life. And I'm sure there are lottery winners who never saved a dime, ignored every financial principle known to man, and who are now set for life. But I don't really consider that retirement planning. Do you?

Surely you realize that the exceptions to the rules get all the press. Why? Because they are the *exceptions*. And if you want to shoot for being an exception to the rule, go right ahead. But why? Why run the risk? Why not live, instead, as if life is connected? The guy who lucks out financially but who ignores the principle of the path relationally still arrives at an undesirable place in his relationships. Beating the odds in one area is no guarantee about anything else.

I don't know the story behind the public events of Vick's unfortunate saga, but I did read one article that may give us some insight. Vick was reluctant to cut his ties with an unhealthy circle of friends. Nothing new there. We've all done that. According to Vick's mentor, James "Poo" Johnson (the assistant chief executive officer of the Boys and Girls Club back in Vick's hometown), Vick had been forewarned about the potential consequences of associating with certain people. In other words, someone had given him a heads-up that trouble was on the horizon. Vick has apologized to his friends, fans, and family. Many have come forward and expressed their support and forgiveness. But he still has to serve his time. For now, that is his destination. When you see danger on the horizon, do something. Take refuge. Whether it's your finances, the condition of your marriage, the way you discipline your kids, relational patterns, moral standards, health care—you name it—if you ignore this principle, there will come a time when all of your options are bad ones.

Every white-water kayaker will tell you the time to scout a rapid is when you are a safe distance away. Only a fool would ignore the Danger! Rapids Ahead sign posted by a state forestry service. Experienced kayakers know that regardless of how calm the water is where you are, you should exit the river to check out what's ahead. Current conditions are not a trustworthy indicator of what lies ahead. Once you hear the thunder of the falls, feel the spray, and see the tops of trees at eye level, you are committed. Your destination is at hand.

What's true for navigating a white-water river applies to navigating your life as well. Ignore the signs, and pay the price. When it dawns on you that you're addicted, that's not the time to start thinking about more accountability and increased discipline. It is too late for that. When your credit cards are full and you are afraid to check the answering machine, that's not the time to consider developing a budget and altering your spending habits. When your spouse serves you with papers, that's not the time to begin working on your marriage. That opportunity is in the rearview mirror. When the pregnancy test reads positive, that's not the time to start reevaluating the soundness of your moral compass or whether he's really the right guy for you.

Assuming that you are ready to abandon the way of the simple to join the ranks of the prudent, I want to close this chapter by giving you something to do and two things to expect. I'll cover them one at a time.

WHAT TO DO

The prudent see danger and take refuge. That is, they *do* something about it. As we stated earlier, they act on what they see.

Prudent people know that it's what you *do* that makes the difference, not what you see. Seeing danger and doing nothing doesn't accomplish anything. Now, that may seem so obvious that you wonder why I bother to state it. But as a preacher, I live in a world of nodding heads and note takers who walk right out the door every Sunday and do very little with what they've heard. And I don't take it personally; we've all done that. We listen, agree, feel convicted, buy the CD, subscribe to the podcast, and take no action. We see trouble coming, and we keep right on going.

If there is going to be change, you must take refuge. You've got to do something. Seeing it, feeling it, agreeing with it is not enough. You are going to need to make a phone call. Have an awkward but honest conversation with a friend. Cut up some credit cards. Change your phone number. Break up. Move out. Find a new circle of friends. Cut back on your traveling. Set the alarm clock on Sunday morning. Empty the liquor cabinet. Join a twelve-step group. Take your family on vacation. Make an appointment with a counselor. Sell the house. Cancel your Internet service. Change jobs. Sell the TV. Maybe all of the above.

Sound extreme? It is. But you know people who would give anything to be able to rewind their lives and do any number of those things if that's what it took to avoid the circumstances in which they now find themselves. I know guys who wish they had never owned a computer. I know couples who wish they had sold their homes when they had a choice, rather than wait until their financial paths left them with no choice. I know employers who wish they could turn back the clock and respond differently to that voice inside their heads that whispered, *Don't hire her.* There are all kinds of actions that feel extreme now that will look like common sense when you are looking back. What feels like a sacrifice now will feel like an investment later on.

What to Expect

Once you determine to act on what you see, you can expect two things: embarrassment and relief. Embarrassment because it will appear to the simple around you that you are overreacting. In an effort to be wise, you may appear to be foolish, even fearful. But the prudent don't react to what they see in their current situations. They react to what they see on the horizon. For those in your circle of friends and family who are accustomed to looking no further than next weekend, you will appear to be a bit . . . odd. Or overly cautious. Acting prudently often appears to others as unnecessary caution. You look a bit silly *now* because you are taking steps to avoid something *later*. To the wise, *later* is *now*. There will always be those who will not understand. In some instances, they don't even want to understand. To admit that your decision makes sense is to admit that they have chosen the wrong path themselves. And their unwillingness to "get it" may eventually cause you to second-guess the wisdom of your decision. Since they think you are crazy, you may begin to wonder yourself. But time will tell.

I have an acquaintance named Buddy who built a forty-thousand-dollar, double-sided, fully lit industrial billboard in the middle of a forest. I'm talking about the kind you see on the interstate. Even in the winter, when the trees shed their leaves, you could barely see it from the nearest road. Anybody who noticed the billboard through the foliage would have thought, *What idiot did that?*

For two years the billboard stood there as a monument to Buddy's seeming stupidity. But eventually the big yellow machines came that way to clear the land for the proposed highway—and this particular stretch of highway was legally deemed a billboard-free zone. But Buddy was there first, so the DOT had to grandfather him in. Now he owns the only billboard on one of the most heavily traveled stretches of highway in Atlanta. Perhaps the most ironic part of the story is that the Georgia Lottery has been leasing one side of his sign since it went up several years ago. So every week, thousands of Georgians who have chosen as part of their financial path an activity synonymous with shredding cash ensure that my friend Buddy receives a big, fat check every month. I'm thinking he's been amply rewarded for the two years he looked a bit foolish. And that leads me to the second thing you can expect when you embrace the principle of the path: relief.

The prudent take refuge and eventually breathe a sigh of relief. The simple, on the other hand, do not. You may have heard someone say, "Pay now, play later." There's a lot of truth in that. The challenge, of course, is that you may have to pay for months. Maybe years. But it will be worth it. The day will come when you'll look back and think, *What if I hadn't acted wisely? What if I had chosen the easy path? What if I hadn't made the decision to end that relationship, confront my boss, fire that manager, sell the house?* But because you took refuge, you will breathe a sigh of relief. You saw trouble and you responded appropriately.

A CLOSE CALL

In 1995, Sandra and I had the opportunity to go sailing with two other couples on one of those all-inclusive packages that included the boat, a skipper, and a cook. We traveled down around St. Thomas for about five days. The weather was picture-perfect. The food was excellent. It was one of those vacations I'll never forget . . . for several reasons.

On our last night, our skipper motored us around into a big, beautiful cove, unspoiled by houses, buildings, or the usual signs of civilization. That is, with the exception of several other boats and a handful of folks waterskiing across the pristine emerald blue-green water.

He backed the boat up about twenty feet from the giant mangrove roots that lined the shore and then tied four lines off the back of our boat. Four. That was a bit strange, since in previous nights he had simply dropped an anchor off the bow out in the middle of a cove and let the breeze carry us around until the boat sat still in the water. But the four stern lines were just the beginning.

While we were swimming and enjoying the time of our lives, the skipper slipped into his scuba gear—not just the snorkel, but the full scuba setup. He dropped a gigantic anchor off the bow, dove in, and physically swam the anchor out a couple of hundred feet. There he manually set it with a chain and rope, then he returned to the boat to do the second thing again, this time with the smaller, second anchor.

But he still wasn't finished. Grabbing several hundred feet of rope, he tied it to the bow of the boat and then, using the dinghy, rowed across the cove and tied it off there. We were all thinking, *What's gotten into Popeye all of a sudden?* If you had happened into our cove at that moment, you would have seen this sixty-five-foot sailboat sitting in glassy water with eight lines out. No doubt you would have thought, *That person knows nothing about sailing. He sure went to a whole lot of trouble for nothing.*

But fortunately our skipper had been listening to the weather report. Hurricane Marilyn was barreling her way toward the Caribbean, packing winds of up to 125 miles per hour and gusts to over 140. The storm had taken an unexpected turn the night before, leaving our island paradise unprepared for what was about to transpire. And unfortunately for us, every tourist in the area was trying to evacuate, so there was no way we could leave. And because the weather changed so quickly, our skipper wasn't sure we could outrun it. Honestly, the idea of trying to outrun a hurricane in a sailboat? So we had no choice but to ride it out. And ride it out we did.

By eight o'clock the skies darkened, the wind picked up, and the rain began to fall. By nine o'clock the rain wasn't falling down anymore. It was falling sideways.

My buddies and I stayed up all night listening to the short-wave radio, shining the skipper's Q-Beam around the cove to see how the other boats were faring, and monitoring the digital wind speed readout on the dashboard. In spite of our six lines and two anchors, the wind gusts would literally heave our boat over to the side enough to force all of us to hold on to the sides of our chairs until they subsided. Around midnight the readout froze at 126 miles per hour. The skipper informed us that the measuring device had probably blown off the mast, which we discovered later it had.

Throughout the night we listened as the police and firemen on St. John and St. Thomas called in damage reports. Two fire stations were destroyed. Hundreds of boats sank. The hospital on St. Thomas had to be evacuated during the night. In the end, this category three storm caused $1.5 billion in damage and killed eight people. Oh yeah, and did I mention that Sandra was five months pregnant with our daughter?

The next morning we went out to survey the damage. In our cove, a boat had been lifted up onto the shore and was left with a hole in the side large enough to walk through. In the cove next to ours, there were a half dozen masts sticking out of the water, the hulls of the boats resting on the bottom. Only then did I realize how afraid I should have been the night before. But actually, none of us was really ever afraid. Why? Great faith? Not really. We saw our skipper prepare for what he knew was coming. He ignored the beautiful afternoon in order to prepare us for the danger that was brewing. He literally saw danger and took refuge. And there are six of us who are very grateful that he did. We are thankful that he didn't take his cue from the other boat owners. We are glad he didn't allow himself to be fooled by the calm before the storm.

Around five o'clock the next day, we motored out of the cove. We were the only ones who did. I'm not sure why the other boat owners weren't better prepared; I can only speculate. But they sure paid a high price for their decision.

PERSONALLY SPEAKING

I won't insult your intelligence by drawing the parallel between our sailing adventure and the point of this chapter. It's pretty obvious. So I'll close with a prayer our family has been praying for many years, a prayer that came directly from this short Proverb:

Lord, help us to see trouble coming long before it gets here. And give us the wisdom to know what to do and the courage to do it. (27:12)

We've been praying that for twenty years. During that time there have been three major events in our marriage when God answered this prayer in unmistakable ways. Early in our marriage, Sandra came to me and said she was troubled by an individual whose motives she had begun to suspect. Her words were, "I think I see trouble coming." I had been sensing the same thing. So we made a decision that didn't make sense to anyone around us. They were baffled. Some were critical. A couple of people were hurt. All we could do was apologize for hurting them, but we could not give them a reason why we had done what we did. I don't think we could have explained it to their satisfaction anyway. But that was a decision we've never regretted.

So I continue to pray every day, "Lord, help us to see trouble coming long before it gets here, and give us the wisdom to know what to do and the courage to do it."

I pray it over our marriage, our finances, our children. I even pray this regarding our children's friends. Like you, I don't always know where a specific path leads. The destination isn't always clear. But when we are given an early warning sign, that's our cue to act. To do something. To take refuge. And there will be awkward moments. There will be decisions that even those closest to you will never fully understand. But in the end there will be relief. In the end you will have avoided unnecessary regret.

Life is short. The seasons of life pass quickly. And each season is connected to the one that follows. Today's decisions create tomorrow's experiences.

My hope is that as you transition from season to season, you will do so with a sigh of relief rather than the pain of regret. For that to be, you must pay attention to what's out ahead of you. When you see trouble coming, take refuge. Change direction. Because it is the direction of your life that will determine your destination.

FIVE

THE HEART
OF THE MATTER

The principle of the path is so obvious, I hesitated even writing about it.

Anyone with half a brain knows that paths have destinations. But even the whole-brain people I know have a chapter or two of their lives they regret. Actually, I should be more forthcoming: I've got a few detours in my past that I regret. And I've got a brain. In fact, my momma assured me on countless occasions that I have a good head on my shoulders. Then she would follow up with something along the lines of, "I wish you would use it occasionally." And she was right. I graduated with a better-than-average GPA from a state university. I graduated with honors from graduate school. People sit in rows and listen to me talk every Sunday. I'm way ahead of Dorothy's scarecrow. But I have done some really stupid things. My greatest regrets are all my fault. Every one of 'em. They stem from decisions I made with my better-than-average brain. And I'm not alone. You've got your stories. Everybody has tales of temporary brain loss. Some are funny. Some represent defining moments—we've never been the same since. Some were close calls. And some were tragic. And looking back, most could have been avoided . . . if we had used our allotment of gray matter a bit more judiciously.

I thought about naming this book *Why Bad Things Happen to Smart People*. You would think that at some point on the IQ scale, the human species would quit making decisions that lead to regret. It seems like we should outgrow the propensity to make stupid decisions. But we don't. And the reason we don't is the topic of this chapter.

Our problem rarely stems from a lack of information or insight. It's something else. Something we don't outgrow. Something that another academic degree won't resolve. Our problem stems from the fact that we are not on a *truth quest*. That is, we don't wake up every morning with a burning desire to know what's true, what's right, what's honorable. We are on a happiness quest. We want to be—as in *feel*—happy. And our quest for happiness often trumps our appreciation for and pursuit of what's true.

Now, I can understand why you may take exception to that. But stay with me for just a couple more pages while I make my case. Let's start with the coffee drinkers. What is that all about? My coffee of choice costs about four bucks a cup. That's ridiculous. Inexcusable in light of the needs in the world today. That's eighty dollars a month if I skip weekends. I could sponsor two more kids through Compassion International for less than that. What's wrong with me? Well, I'm on a happiness quest. And soy lattes contribute to my happiness. In fact, as I learned a few years ago when I quit drinking coffee for a few months, my soy lattes contribute to the happiness of my staff as well. I actually had a key staff member call me aside and tell me in no uncertain terms that I was more fun to be around when I was drinking coffee. That's all the excuse I needed.

If you have perfectly good clothes you never wear hanging in your closet but you plan to do a little shopping later this week, what's that about? Why would you buy more clothes when you don't wear the ones you have? Answer: Because when you wear something new and stylish, you feel better about yourself. Happy. When you put on last year's model, you feel a bit last-yearish. Unhappy. And you don't want to feel that way. So when you head for the mall, you aren't simply shopping for clothes. You are in search of the happy feeling that comes with looking good.

Have you ever traded in (or *accidentally* dropped) a perfectly good cell phone for a newer model? Do you own an iPhone? Did you spend a ridiculous amount of time and energy trying to finagle your way out of your old contract so that you could get a specific phone your carrier didn't provide? Have you carried two contracts for a while because you just couldn't wait?

I'll save cars and trucks for later. But you get the point. As smart as we are and as aware as we are that life is connected and that decisions today shape the experiences of tomorrow, we still don't wake up in the morning in search of truth, insight, and enlightenment. We get up and do the things that make us happy. We are all on a happiness quest. And I don't think that is necessarily wrong. Fortunately, there is a great deal of overlap between doing what's right and wise and doing what makes us happy. For example, my wife loves to exercise. And that makes *me* happy. But that's not really the point, is it? Exercise—something that is good for my wife's current and future health—is something she enjoys. So in that case, pursuing something that makes her happy is a good thing. But she would be quick to tell you that chocolate makes her happy as well. Happier than exercise. Pursuing that happy-path every day would not be a good thing. It's these forks in the road—or for our purposes, forks in the path—that make things complicated. When happiness points in one direction while wisdom, truth, integrity, and common sense point in another, that's when really smart people start doing really stupid things. That's when the happiness quest becomes dangerous. This is the underlying reason we intentionally choose paths that will not take us to where we ultimately want to go, regardless of our SAT scores.

HERE TODAY, HERE TOMORROW

The problem with the happiness quest is that happy today does not necessarily equal happy tomorrow. Decisions and experiences that fill me with happiness today may very well fill me with regret tomorrow. The thing I pursued with reckless abandon today may be the thing I try to escape from tomorrow, and in some cases, pay an attorney a lot of money to help me escape from tomorrow. Happy is schizophrenic. My friends who are trying to quit smoking started smoking because it was fun. They enjoyed it. It was relaxing and helped them keep the weight off. Now, the very thing they enjoyed, they hate. And they wish that when they were standing at the fork in the path years ago, they had opted for prudent over happy. If they had, they would be happier now.

If you are carrying credit card debt that is so old you don't even remember what it was for anymore, you know what it is like to stand at that fork in the path. In fact, the salespeople who helped you get in that hole made it perfectly clear that you had a choice to make. Remember what they said? "Cash or credit?" Or perhaps, "Credit or debit?" It would have helped if they had said, "Happy later or happy now?" And remember how fun it was to go home with new stuff? Those were happy moments. But now the stuff is . . . heck, you don't even know where all that stuff is. But you aren't happy about it anymore.

Spending is just one arena. We eat because it makes us happy. Then one day we look in the mirror and what we see makes us sick. So we diet and exercise ourselves back into shape. And *that* makes us happy. Perhaps you stood at a fork in the path relationally. Your upbringing whispered, "Don't move in." But Happy Now whispered, "Start packing and hope your parents don't find out." And you played house for a couple of months or years and one day realized you weren't really happy anymore. Hmm. So you moved out. And then you were happy again. But you realized you would be even happier if you had never gotten involved in that unhappy relationship that "Happy Now" talked you into.

60

TELL ME SOMETHING I DON'T KNOW ALREADY

As you are reading all this, I doubt you are thinking, *This guy is brilliant. I never saw any of this before.* More than likely you are thinking, *Okay, okay, I get it. But why? Why do I opt for short-term happiness over long-term happiness? Why do I have to have my way now rather than wait and really have my way later? Why do I knowingly choose paths that take me where I've already decided I don't want to go?*

The answer is, when we stand at the crossroads between prudent and happy, we lie to ourselves. We turn into dishonest salespeople. We begin selling ourselves on what we *want* to do rather than what we *ought* to do. We listen to ourselves until we believe our own lies, and then we opt for happiness. It's really a strange thing. That brain we thought should keep us out of trouble becomes part of the problem. Because once we get fixated on the happiness option, we assign our brains the task of coming up with a list of very convincing reasons to support our choice. Reasons, by the way, that really have nothing to do with why we chose to do what we did.

Another way of saying the same thing is that we listen to our hearts, and then we assign our heads the responsibility of building a case to support our hearts' decisions. But again, the reasons *follow* the decisions—they aren't the real reasons behind our decisions.

Confused? Perhaps a couple of illustrations would help. Let's talk about cars. Think about reasons you've used to support your decision to trade in a perfectly good car for a newer model. While you think about yours, I'll tell you about my friend Chuck. Chuck traded in his wife's perfectly good SUV for a newer one. When I saw it, I said, "Hey, Chuck, I see you got your wife a new ride."

Now, if he were honest, he would have said, "Yeah, the new one looks better, smells better, has a Bluetooth and some smokin' hot twenty-inch wheels." Or he could have given me the really short, ultra-honest answer, "Yeah, I got it because when I saw it, I wanted it." But instead he said, "Yeah, the other one was eatin' us alive with the poor gas mileage. This one is more fuel efficient."

Now, I didn't buy that for a minute. You don't trade SUVs for fuel efficiency. Besides, he will probably trade again before his potential savings catches up with what he spent on his new transportation. But don't be too hard on Chuck. Chuck is like the rest of us. Once he made a happiness/heart decision, he told his brain to come up with something good to justify it. Unfortunately, fuel efficiency was all his brain could come up with.

Granted, it's hard to ruin your life by lying to yourself about a single car purchase. But extend that same dynamic over a decade of purchases and you may arrive at a destination you never intended to visit. One thing that makes it so difficult not to lie to ourselves in the arena of purchasing and finances is that we get so much help from culture.

- Zero percent financing!
- Deferred financing!
- No money down!
- Don't pay a thing until Christmas!
- Now more affordable than ever!
- You owe it to yourself!
- Free upgrades!

If you can't come up with a good justification for your financial decisions, just ask the guy or gal behind the counter or on the other end of the telephone. Someone will always help you out. But most of the time we really don't need outside help.

Several years ago Sandra and I built a house on a piece of property we had owned for a few years. By normal standards it's a big house. There are larger houses around, but ours is larger than average. From time to time people who had driven by and seen it would walk up and say, "Hey, Andy, we saw your house. Pretty big." As you would imagine, we started to feel a bit self-conscious, so what do you suppose we did? We sent our brains on a justification safari. We felt compelled to come up with a reasonable explanation to deflect the embarrassment. When asked about the house, we'd say things like, "Well, you know, we like to entertain, and we enjoy using it for ministry purposes." Now, both of those things are true. We entertain a lot, and we host a community group in our home on Sunday nights. But that's not *why* we built the size house we did. Those are just the reasons our brains produced to support a happiness decision. And I guarantee you that nobody bought our lame excuses anyway. We built our house the size it is because . . . because that's what we *wanted* to do. That's what made us happy. It was not about *need*. It was all about *want*.

Gee, I feel better having gotten that out.

Here's the strange thing. Even though we didn't do anything wrong, we still felt the need to make excuses for our decision rather than just admitting to ourselves and others that this was an I-did-it-'cause-I-wanted-to decision. And this is my point: our propensity to defend our happiness decisions with justifications that aren't founded in truth is what sets us up for trouble when the road divides. You can't have it both ways when prudence veers one way and happiness-right-now veers the other.

Breaking 'Em Up Is Hard to Do

Through the years I've tried to talk dozens of people out of getting married. Not getting married in general, but marrying a particular person. In these extreme situations I feel like these precious individuals are standing at a fork in the path. From my vantage point, prudence is whispering, "Run away," while happiness shouts, "Take me to the chapel! Now!" In each of these situations there were plenty of practical reasons why these particular couples should not marry. From debt to anger to differing value systems to unresolved issues from previous relationships. But on the other side of the equation is always love. "But I love her." Somehow love always trumped my observations, insights, experience, and principles.

I have a friend named Susan who taught me a good response to "I love her." She says, "Yeah, but what do you love *about* her?" I wish I had heard that a long time ago. "What do I love *about* her (or him)" has a way of throwing the discussion back to the more sensible side of life. But regardless of how sensible I was, I rarely made any progress with these couples. Love conquers all—including prudence and common sense. Time after time I sat and watched as couples turned a blind eye to the things that would doom their marriages before they began. Self-deception is easy when emotions run high. And nothin' runs 'em higher than love. So they would side with the happiness impulse and then send their brains on a search for justification. And the justifications were so weak. "It'll work out." "We won't let that happen in our relationship." "We'll be careful." Then off they would go, running down a path that I knew would not take them to a destination they anticipated or desired. And the interesting thing is this: many of those couples who left my office, angry with me for not marrying them, came running right back to me when things went south. And I never said it, though I often thought it: *Why don't you go see the bozo who took your two hundred bucks and tied this poorly tied knot in the first place?* Oh well . . .

Our problem is rarely a lack of information or insight. It's not that we fail to see trouble brewing on the horizon. It's a lack of honesty. We have a hard time leveling with ourselves. We deceive ourselves about why we choose the things we choose. And then we spin a web of excuses to protect ourselves, excuses that over time we come to believe.

So married guys tell themselves that the reason they keep stopping by the cute intern's cube is to make sure she has everything she needs to do her job. And singles tell themselves that they are sharing an apartment with their significant other for financial reasons. And alcoholics tell themselves they can stop drinking whenever they want to. And businesspeople tell themselves that there is no way to reduce their travel schedules and that they are not avoiding issues at home. And teenagers tell themselves that they are maintaining unhealthy relationships in order to be a friend. And everyone represented by each of those examples is on a path. A path that does not lead to where they want to go—but one they continue to walk in part because they refuse to be honest with themselves. Like all of us at some stage of our journeys, they offer up reasons that aren't really *the* reason.

WHAT YOU WON'T KNOW WILL HURT YOU

As long as we are lying to ourselves, it is impossible to get to where we want to be. Here's why. You will never get to where you want to be if you don't know where you are to begin with. When we deceive ourselves, we blind ourselves to our current location. Maps are useless if you don't know where you are. This reminds me of a friend's son who got lost driving by himself at night for the first time. When he realized he didn't know where he was, he grabbed his cell phone and called his dad. His dad started questioning him about what he saw around him so as to get some idea of where he might be. But that turned out to be a mistake. His son started looking for landmarks instead of paying attention to the road. Suddenly he looked up and the car in front of him was stopped. To avoid an accident he drove off onto the shoulder of the road and into a shallow ditch. He wasn't hurt, but he *was* stuck. When his dad realized he was okay, he said, "Don't worry, son, I'll come get you out. Just tell me where you are." Long pause. "Dad, that's the point. I don't have any idea where I am."

Geographically speaking, you can't get to where you want to be unless you know where you are to begin with. You need a reference point. Similarly, you can't get to where you want to be in life until you are willing to admit where you are to begin with. Self-deception makes that next to impossible. Think about it for a moment. Don't all the lies you tell yourself have a similar theme?

- Everything is fine.

- Everything is going to work out.

- I'll get through this.

- I can handle this.

- It's all going to be all right.

That kind of self-talk doesn't help when you are lost on the highway. And it doesn't help when you are lost in life. All that does is empower you to keep moving in the wrong direction. Those messages are the very messages that keep a person from stopping and getting help.

To find the path that will take you where you want to go, you must break the cycle of self-deception. As long as you hide behind reasons that aren't the real reasons for your behavior, you will never have the clarity or strength you need to turn around and move in a new direction.

LIVE AND LEARN

So why are we prone toward self-deception? Why do we lie to ourselves? If you are over eighteen, you've lived long enough to know that it doesn't lead anywhere good. Your personal, financial, and relational experiences probably back up everything I've said in this chapter. So what's up?

Perhaps the best and most succinct answer to our question came from the lips of the Old Testament prophet Jeremiah. Jeremiah served as God's mouthpiece to Israel's kings around

600 BC. One of those kings was Jehoiakim. When he took the throne, he began steering the nation toward the pagan practices of her neighbors. These were dark days for Jeremiah. Time after time he warned the new king of the dangers of breaking Israel's covenant with God. He told him that unless he repented, God would allow the armies of Babylon to overrun the city of Jerusalem. But the king wouldn't listen. Over time Jeremiah's words created a sense of panic among the people in Jerusalem. So the king had Jeremiah arrested. When Jeremiah continued to prophesy gloom and doom from his place of incarceration, the king had him put in a cistern to shut him up. Jeremiah was still under arrest when, in 588 BC, the city fell to the invaders from the north.

Jeremiah had watched in disbelief as king Jehoiakim ignored his nation's history and the events surrounding his rule, as well as a direct warning from God. He watched as the king continued down a path that even a uninformed observer could see would end in the destruction of the city. Sometime during these chaotic events, the aging prophet arrived at the following conclusion:

The heart is deceitful above all things and beyond cure. (Jer. 17:9)

That's a pretty broad stroke. *The* heart, as in *every heart,* is deceitful. And beyond cure. As you know, there's a difference between dishonest and deceitful. You've met dishonest people who were not shrewd enough to deceive you. Their dishonesty was so apparent that you didn't buy it; you didn't fall for anything. But deceitfulness is different. It is one thing to be lied to. It is quite another to be tricked and led astray. Jeremiah's words were carefully chosen. The heart doesn't simply lie. Our hearts are deceitful. Our hearts have the ability to lead us astray.

If Jeremiah was right, we would do well to abandon the adage, *Trust your heart.* Apparently, the heart can't be trusted. And based on our observations thus far, Jeremiah's words explain a lot. If our hearts are deceitful by nature, then it is no wonder we are so prone to deceive ourselves. It comes naturally. Perhaps that's why we are so convinced and at times are so convincing. It's coming right out of our hearts. We aren't merely lying to ourselves; we are genuinely deceived.

Jeremiah's words don't leave us with a lot of hope: ". . . and beyond cure." There's no cure? No magic pill? No special prayer? No seminar, conference, or book that can fix it? But that wasn't the end. Look where he went next:

The heart is deceitful above all things and beyond cure. Who can understand it? (Jer. 17:9)

How many times have you looked back on something you've done and thought, *I don't understand why I did that. What was I thinking?* Think of the times you've watched smart people do dumb things and thought, *I don't understand why they would do that. What were they thinking?* The reason you don't understand some of your decisions is the same reason I don't understand many of mine. According to Jeremiah, nobody can understand the heart.

The heart is incurably deceitful. It's untrustworthy. Dishonest.

Corrupt. Consequently, you and I will always have the ability—even the propensity—to lie to ourselves, act on those lies, and then defend the lies with loopy excuses.

7 THE WORK-AROUND

If all of that is true, it explains a lot, but it doesn't leave us with many options. But though we are powerless to fix our hearts, we don't have to be slaves to them. Once you know you can't trust somebody, it is easier to ignore his pitch, regardless of how convincing it sounds. Once you settle on the fact that your heart can't be trusted, it becomes easier to pause and evaluate before charging down whatever path your heart urges you to follow.

One of Jesus' most often quoted statements addresses this head-on:

And you shall know the truth, and the truth shall make you free. (John 8:32 NKJV)

The truth is, your heart can't always be trusted. The truth is, there are better decision-making strategies than simply following your heart. The truth is, if you let it, your heart will direct you down a path that leads to the very spot you most want to avoid. And now that you know the *truth* about your heart, you don't have to be deceived! You can live free of self-deception. You don't have to spend the next season of your life trying to untangle yourself from decisions you made in this season. You won't have to spend another sleepless night trying to understand why you did what you did.

Because now you *know* something you didn't know before. Namely, your heart should not be your guide. It can't be trusted.

Fessin' Up

At the beginning of this chapter, we discussed our propensity to go looking for sound reasons to support our unsound decisions. That's what happens when your brain is taking orders from your heart. The heart says, "You owe it to yourself to borrow more than you should to drive something you can't afford." Then your brain goes looking for an explanation you can use with your friends: gas mileage, fewer miles, safety, end-of-year closeout, and so on. But when you decide to quit taking cues from your heart, your brain has a new role. Now instead of looking for excuses to prop up your heart decisions, your brain starts looking for the *real* reason you want to do things. And by examining the real reason, you will free yourself from the deceptive power of your heart. But this isn't easy. Most of us have been excusing our bad decisions for a long time. It is hard to tell ourselves the truth. It is hard not to revert to using our brains to support our hearts. But once you decide to get painfully honest with yourself, it can be extraordinarily liberating.

I know a woman who married her husband for his money. She didn't know it at the time. But I did. Other people did. And I, along with a couple of her friends, did everything I could to get her to admit that before she married him. You should have heard her explanations. It would have been amusing if it weren't so tragic. As convincing as she sounded, she was really the only one who was convinced. And, of course, her ace in the hole was, "But

I love him." I told her I couldn't do the wedding. She was not very happy about that. But her momma seemed to be relieved that I was out of the loop. They were married for five years. Had a cute little boy. Then she filed for divorce. And the reasons she gave for leaving him were the very reasons her friends and I gave her for not marrying him in the first place!

Several years later she came to see me. She was still as angry as the day she filed. All she could talk about was what a jerk he was and how many times she had had to take him to court for child support. The reason she came to see me was related to an impending court date. After thirty or forty minutes of listening, I finally held up my hand and asked, "Why did you marry him?" Her eyes got wide, and she started to say something but stopped. Then she started crying. These weren't anger tears. These were tears of regret. We both knew the answer to that question. And she almost said it. I think I could see the words forming on her lips. She was so close. And if she had just blurted it out—"I married him because he was rich, and I was tired of being single"—if she had just been willing to cross that line of honesty with herself, I think something wonderful would have happened on the inside of her.

I came so close to saying it for her. But I didn't want to accuse. I wanted her to embrace a truth that I'm convinced would have shaved away 50 percent of her rage. She was angry with herself. But she had never admitted it. And as we sat there in my office, I sensed that we were a sentence away from a truth that would have set her free.

After a long pause, I saw the determination return to her face.

And I knew the moment had passed. "Andy," she said, "I know what you are thinking. And I'm not going there." With that, she gathered her things, got up, and walked out of my office. I haven't seen or spoken with her since. Why did she run? Because sometimes truth is so painful we would rather run than embrace it. She didn't want to go "there." "There" was telling herself the truth. And in doing so, it meant taking responsibility for the mess her life had become.

Telling ourselves the truth is liberating, but it can be terrifying.

The real reason I lie about my family is . . .

The real reason I filed for divorce is . . .

The real reason we moved in together was . . .

The real reason I won't call my kids is . . .

The real reason for my credit card debt is . . .

The real reason I drink so much is . . .

The real reason I quit going to church is . . .

When you are willing to come clean with yourself about the uncomfortable truth behind your choices, you're on the verge of freedom. We can never be free as long as we're in the habit of lying to ourselves about the reasons behind the choices we make and the paths we take. Telling yourself the truth will free you to move from where you are to where you want and need to be. As we said earlier, you can't get to where you need to be until you acknowledge where you actually are. As long as we lie to ourselves, we never really know where we are.

As we close this chapter, I want to leave you with three questions that will help you keep your heart in check. But in order for these questions to be effective, you've got to answer them as if no one were going to hold you accountable for your answer . . . not even God. Answer them as if God can't hear your thoughts. This is important because the reason we don't acknowledge the rationale behind our decisions is that if we do, we immediately feel both guilty and accountable. So when answering these questions, you need to do everything you can to take both of those dynamics out of the equation. So, assuming no one will know and that you don't have to act on your answers, answer the following.

1. Why am I doing this, really?
2. If someone in my circumstances came to me for advice, what course of action would I recommend?
3. In light of my past experience, my future hopes, and my dreams, what is the wise thing to do?

Now allow me, if you will, to be a bit facetious. If, after a painfully honest look in the mirror, you decide to do something you would never advise someone in your shoes to do, something unwise, something that will in all probability lead you somewhere you never intended to go, congratulations! You are doing something very few people have the courage to do. You are making a bad decision with your eyes wide open. You are no longer deceived by your heart. You are using your head. And you know exactly what you are getting yourself into. And when you hit a wall, you won't spend the next season of your life blaming others. You will know that you only have yourself to blame. But best of all, by telling yourself the truth, you will know where you are and how to get to where you need to be.

My hope is that by answering those questions honestly, you will be overwhelmed with a clarity you may have otherwise lacked. But not just clarity. Clarity and courage. Clarity to know *what* to do. And *courage* to do it. My hope is that next time you stand at a fork in the path where "happiness now" and "happiness later" point in different directions, you will refuse to be deceived by your heart. And that instead you would lean hard into what you know, and have been willing to admit to yourself, is true.

>> SIX

MY ITALIAN JOB

Not too long ago, Sandra and I had an opportunity to go to Florence, Italy, to celebrate her fortieth birthday. Talk about a cool trip. I mean, Florence dates back to the days of Julius Caesar, who established the city in 59 BC. Everywhere you look and everything you see is just dripping with history.

Joining us on the trip to the cradle of the Renaissance were two dear friends, Doris and Howard Bowen. They, like us, were thrilled to visit the home of Leonardo da Vinci and Michelangelo while sampling the local food.

Now, as I pointed our earlier, I'm terrible with directions. So I thought it would be best if I drove. That way Sandra, Howard, and Doris could act as navigators. No one else seemed eager to take the wheel, so I volunteered. And speaking of navigators, we actually had two—not one—*two* portable GPS devices with our entire trip preprogrammed. So basically there was no possible way for us to get lost. Every three minutes we had two very nice electronic ladies telling us exactly where to turn and, in several instances, when it was time to turn around. Why two? Because we were going to be doubly sure we didn't get lost. So we had one mounted on the dashboard and one in the backseat with Howard.

The trip from the airport to our hotel went off without a hitch. But as we were pulling up in front of the hotel, we realized there was no place to unload. Like many of the streets in Europe, this one was designed for horses, not minivans. If we stopped to unload our luggage, we'd back up traffic. Tossing the bags out the window one at a time as we cruised by didn't sound like a good idea either.

That's when it occurred to me that there must be a back entrance to the hotel, a place where we could actually park and then unload passengers and luggage (with the aid of a bellhop, we hoped). I was determined to find a way to get around back. So for fifteen minutes we went in circles as the GPSs kept sending us back to the front of the building. I got so tired of being lectured by the ladies of GPS that I turned the one in the front off and announced that I was pretty sure I had figured out how to get us to the back of the hotel. After all, I'd been driving for thirty years. I'd seen *The Italian Job*—twice. Granted, that movie was in Venice, not Florence, but they were both in Italy. So I took over and did it my way.

I could tell my three passengers didn't share my confidence. Howard actually left his GPS device on. Sandra pulled out the map. Meanwhile, I just drove. Fast.

Within a few minutes, Sandra pointed out something a bit unnerving: there were no cars on the street we were traveling on.

None. Except ours. Instead, we found ourselves wading into a sea of humanity. There were hundreds of people surrounding us. In front of us. Behind us. On all sides of us. Staring. At us.

It didn't take a genius for us to realize that we were driving in an area designed for pedestrian traffic only. But I was unwavering in my determination to get us to the back of the hotel. And I was sure this pedestrian walkway would get us there. While I refused to concede defeat, Sandra, Doris, and Howard were doing their best to avoid eye contact with anybody outside our minivan. Did I mention it was a *Ford* minivan? The only Ford we saw in Italy. Why we were driving an American car in Europe is another story. But suffice it to say we had *tourists* written all over us.

Eventually I came to my senses and realized that not only were we not supposed to be driving in this area but we were also nowhere near our hotel. I needed to turn around, but there were two problems with that plan. The street was too narrow, and we were surrounded by people. There was a street to our right, so I took a chance and made a right turn. About a hundred feet ahead it looked like the street emptied out onto some kind of plaza. So I drove on in hopes that the larger, less congested area would allow me to turn around. As we neared the end of the street, I began to get a sick feeling in my stomach. Sure enough, it was a plaza. One of the most famous plazas in Florence, not to mention one of the top tourist destinations in Europe: the Piazza della Signoria. It was built in the thirteenth century. At one time it was the heart of the city's social and political life. It is lined with some of the most famous statues in the world. And we were parked on it!

I was so overwhelmed, I didn't know what to do. We couldn't

back up or move forward. I just knew any minute we were going to get arrested. So I literally put the minivan into park, got out, closed the door, and just walked off into the crowd. Stunned, my wife and two friends were left sitting in the van, staring at my back. I stood at a distance, looking back at the minivan, wondering how in the heck we were going to turn around and make our way back through the crowds. All the while I was thinking, *I should have trusted the GPS.*

Well, eventually I went back to the van. Sandra and the Bowens were horrified. Nobody was making eye contact with anyone outside the van. We were far too humiliated for that. I began the tedious task of turning the van around in the crowd and slowly making our way back toward our hotel. As it turned out, there really was no rear entrance. We had to stop traffic for twenty minutes while we unloaded our luggage. Then an attendant drove our van away to a parking garage in some other part of town. I was actually pretty happy about that. Fortunately for us, the entire incident turned out to be nothing more than a lesson in humility, a waste of about an hour, and a story to tell. And one more thing . . .

Our little misadventure serves as a perfect segue into the subject of this chapter: the relationship between submission to God and our ability to pick the best path. Now, I realize *submission* is not your favorite word. It's not mine either. *Dove Bar* is actually my favorite word (okay, my favorite two words), but I'm not sure how helpful a chapter on Dove Bars would be. Anyway, my failure to trust—or submit to—our multiple GPS devices is what led to our visit to the plaza. In a similar way, our failure to trust or submit to our heavenly Father will lead to unintended destinations as well. But instead of wasting an hour, those detours can eat up years.

Now and Later

The challenging aspect about picking the right paths is that the choices are *now*. The outcomes are *later*. The decisions you make *today* have ramifications *down the road*. Sometimes the outcomes happen tomorrow: You studied for a test on Tuesday night and did well on Wednesday. You prepped for a presentation to the board yesterday, and it was a hit in the boardroom today.

The problem, however, is that most of the time the outcome of our decision won't be felt until later. Much later. The path you chose in high school—to apply yourself and study hard in order to make good grades, or to play hooky and have a good time—impacts your destination in college. The paths you chose in your twenties as a single person impact what happens to you in your thirties when you're married with kids. The financial path you chose early on in your marriage to spend or save impacts what happens financially as you face retirement.

Unfortunately, you and I don't know the outcome of many decisions we make until it's too late to do anything about it. Sure, sometimes we're glad. Oftentimes we're disappointed—or worse, devastated. Regardless of the outcome, one thing is certain: we cannot go back in time, reset the clock, and recapture those years. They're gone. There's no way to unmake those decisions—which is why it's so crucial for us to make the right decisions up front.

But how?

Like I said, we make choices today and won't know the effects of those choices for years or decades. There's a delayed reaction between the first cigarette at fifteen and emphysema at fifty; between the casual sex as a teen and cervical cancer or infertility at thirty; or, on a more positive note, between the habit of investing in an IRA in your twenties and retiring with plenty of money in the bank at sixty.

Some of those outcomes are obvious because of the abundance of available data. For example, the Surgeon General's warning on every pack of cigarettes. Or think back to that uncomfortable day in health class when your teacher discussed STDs. If you were real lucky, there was a slide show to go along with the lecture.

Frequently, however, we face decisions where the outcomes aren't so clear-cut. If only someone had a Web site containing a database with all of the possible choices and their probable outcomes based upon the experiences of millions of people over a few hundred years.

That'd be cool.

I mean, imagine the ability to research the dating and marriage decisions made by others and then study their outcomes. Or the ability to learn from a host of financial, parenting, and professional decisions made by others. That way we'd know the statistical odds of where specific decisions lead. Armed with such a gold mine of information, we'd always make the right decision and choose the best path, right?

Probably not.

For starters, we probably wouldn't follow the advice. We would assume, as we often do, that we are the exception to all those statistics.

Take, for instance, Ed and Linda. Married for two decades, this couple sat in my office on the verge of bankruptcy and divorce. Their financial woes had begun ten years prior to our meeting. When they sensed things weren't moving in the right direction, they made a very wise decision. They made an appointment with a financial planner. He created a plan that was tailored to their specific situation. It included a debt-reduction schedule and long-term savings goals. He helped them develop a budget, and he suggested a couple of books to read that he felt would motivate them to work their plan. Then he put the whole thing in a nifty little binder and sent them on their way. As they recounted their story, they both acknowledged how hopeful they'd felt that day as they drove home. For the first time in their marriage, they had a plan.

So why, then, were they sitting in my office, drowning in red ink?

Upon arriving at home with their ticket to financial freedom, Ed put the binder in a drawer and never looked at it again. It wasn't that he and Linda didn't agree with the plan. On the contrary, they thought it was a great plan; very doable. They just never "doabled" it.

Let's face it: we've all ignored good advice at some point in our lives. We've ignored advice from doctors, professional coaches, physical therapists, motivational speakers, nutritionists, preachers, marriage counselors, friends, even our mothers-in-law. The list goes on and on. And the embarrassing thing is, in most cases we paid for the advice we ignored! Looking back, our lives would be richer today had we done something with what we heard.

If good information isn't enough to guarantee good decisions, then what do we need? What are we missing?

I'm glad I asked.

Choosing the right path begins with *submission*, not information. Not even direction. Submission. Specifically, submission to the One who knows where each path leads, as well as where it doesn't lead. Submission to the One who knows what's best for you better than *you* know what's best for you.

It is tempting to think that information alone is enough. You have your own illustrations to prove that it is not. Generally speaking, information is not our problem. There's plenty of that. Independence is our problem. And the solution for independence is the dreaded *S* word: submission. When you and I get ahead of God—by thinking we can do just fine without his direction or by relying solely on conventional wisdom—things don't go so well. The problem, of course, is that sometimes it takes years, some of our best years, to discover that we have made a mistake. Thus the infamous parental line: *Do as I say, not as I did.*

THE SMARTEST MAN IN THE ROOM

If ever there was a man who could have trusted in his own ability to discern which path to choose, it was King Solomon. The Bible refers to Solomon as the wisest man who ever lived. Heck, he wrote three books in the Bible: Proverbs (well worth reading ASAP), Ecclesiastes (don't read until you're over forty), and Song of Solomon (only read after you're married . . . or if you think the Bible is boring).

Inside those books (which, by the way, we refer to as *wisdom literature*), Solomon displayed his remarkable insight into all realms of science, mathematics, business, marriage, and justice. Name the topic, and his wealth of understanding was unequaled. But this wasn't the result of being born to smart parents. Solomon's insight was due in great part to God's unique intervention in his life. Perhaps you've heard the story.

When Solomon assumed the throne in the place of his father, David, he was around twenty years old. David had been a great warrior. Solomon was a great . . . well, we don't know that he was great at anything. So we shouldn't be surprised to discover that he felt a bit overwhelmed with the responsibility of leading his nation. Not to mention his dad left him with the responsibility of building a temple. And not just *a* temple. *The* temple. The *first* temple. And supposedly, the *only* temple the nation would ever have. And as far as we know, Solomon didn't know the first thing about construction.

As Solomon was settling into his royal role, God communicated to him in a dream. To paraphrase, God said, "Solomon, because I loved your father, I love you; and because I made a promise to your father, I want to make a promise to you. Ask me anything you want. Just make a request and I'll give it to you. You want long life, you got it. You want money, no problem."

Solomon had a blank check.

Imagine that. What would you have asked for at twenty?

Solomon asked for wisdom. Wisdom. And that's a bit odd, because you would already have to have a boatload of wisdom to even come up with that response. Apparently Solomon was just wise enough to know how wise he wasn't. So he asked for more wisdom. Here's how he put it:

Now, O LORD my God, you have made your servant king in place of my father David. But I am only a little child and do not know how to carry out my duties. Your servant is here among the people you have chosen, a great people, too numerous to count or number. So give your servant a discerning heart to govern your people and to distinguish between right and wrong. (1 Kings 3:7–9)

God was so pleased with Solomon's request that he gave him all the stuff I probably would have asked for to begin with:

Since you have asked for this and not for long life or wealth for yourself, nor have asked for the death of your enemies but for discernment in administering justice, I will do what you have asked. I will give you a wise and discerning heart, so that there will never have been anyone like you, nor will there ever be. Moreover, I will give you what you have not asked for—both riches and honor—so that in your lifetime you will have no equal among kings. (1 Kings 3:11–13)

And sure enough, Solomon became extraordinarily wealthy and extremely powerful. There was peace along the borders of Israel. Kings and queens from surrounding nations traveled great distances to come and sit at his feet and listen. In time, Solomon's kingdom was the envy of the ancient world. Many refer to this as the Golden Age of Israel.

My point? If ever there was a person who could say, "God, now that I've got the wisdom I need and access to all the available information, feel free to go and do whatever God does because I've got everything I need to call my own shots. You are hereby dismissed. I can take it from here," it'd be Solomon.

But Solomon was wise enough to know better. He knew wisdom and information alone were not enough. Wisdom and information didn't guarantee anything. Even he knew better than to trust in his judgment alone. Later in life he would offer this advice to anyone wise enough to listen:

> Trust in the LORD with all your heart, and lean not on your own understanding. (Prov. 3:5)

That's pretty straightforward, isn't it? Don't trust your heart; trust God *with* your heart. The term translated *trust* carried with it the idea of lying helplessly facedown. Vulnerable. Dependent. Then notice the contrast. "Lean not" as in "Don't prop yourself up with . . ." The term translated *lean* literally means to prop something up against something else; to be supported by it.

The imagery associated with the term *lean* gives us further insight into what he meant by *trust* in the first half of the verse.

Solomon was instructing us to lean on the Lord rather than lean on our own understanding and insight. When the way we view things conflicts with the way God views things, we are to lean in his direction rather than our own. When what makes sense to us doesn't line up with his revealed will, we are to side with him and ignore the whispers of our hearts.

It's as if he could read our minds. He wrote as if he'd been following us around. Somehow he knew that our propensity was to choose our paths according to how they looked and felt to us. Solomon was saying that in spite of all you know and all you have experienced, don't make the mistake of thinking that you're old enough, wise enough, smart enough, experienced enough, or careful enough to be able to lean on (as in trust) your own understanding.

Choosing the best path, then, begins with submission. When considering our options, the place to begin is, *Lord, I'm leaning on you, not my experience, my insight, or my education. When conventional wisdom conflicts with what you have revealed through the Scriptures, I'll lean hard into your revelation rather than my understanding. When my emotions are in conflict with your law, I'll lean on your law and harness my emotions.*

Obviously, this is easier said than done. But observation and experience would argue that it is much easier in the long run to lean into the wisdom of your heavenly Father than to lean into your own. As our detour through the Piazza della Signoria reminds us, leaning on our own understanding has the potential to take us exactly where we don't want to be and never planned to be. In our case, we lost an hour. But leaning on our own understanding in the arenas of finance, parenting, marriage, or any number of things has the potential to cost us a lot more.

ALL WAYS

Thus far the wisest man in the world has given us two important imperatives: *trust in* and *lean not*. But that's only half the equation. In the second half he gives us a third command and a promise.

> In all your ways acknowledge him, and he will make your paths straight. (Prov. 3:6)

Notice he didn't say, "In *most all* of your ways." He said "all." Solomon didn't leave any wiggle room. *In all your ways* means in your dating ways, your marriage ways, your entertainment ways, your morality ways, your education ways, your professional ways, your financial ways. He wasn't speaking of just your Sunday ways, your religious ways, or your prayer ways. *All* means *all*. In every arena of life, we are to acknowledge God. So what does that mean?

Unfortunately, the word *acknowledge* has lost something over the years. Ever listen to a public speaker, sports figure, or guest of honor at a fund-raising banquet? Typically he'll begin his comments by saying something like, "I'd like to start by acknowledging so-and-so for his blah-blah-blah." But when Solomon used the word *acknowledge*, he wasn't talking about a token tip of the hat or some sort of obligatory shout-out, giving God his props for being a nice guy.

Rather, to acknowledge God means to recognize who he is and respond accordingly. What is the proper response to God? Submission. We are to recognize God's authority over every component of our lives. We are to seek and submit to his will in every area of life. That is, in all our ways.

That said, Solomon concludes with an extremely practical promise: "and he will make your paths straight."

There's our word: *path*. At first glance, it looks as if Solomon is guaranteeing that if we trust God, he will straighten out whatever path we choose. But what this verse actually asserts is that God will make the best path *obvious*. If we trust with all our hearts, refuse to lean into our limited understanding, and submit every aspect of our lives to him, the best path will become unmistakably clear. Divine direction begins with unconditional submission. Not information.

If you think about it, this is exactly what we should expect. If you are familiar at all with the Old Testament, you know that the story line revolves around God's relationship with Israel. If you've read much of the New Testament, you know that Jesus came to pave the way for all mankind to have a personal relationship with God. God who, by the way, has invited us to call him Father. As you read either testament, you come away with the distinct impression that God's primary interest is not that we always make the *right* decisions. "Happily ever after" is not his goal. He wants more. He desires a personal connection. A relationship. And through Christ he has gone to great lengths to make that possible.

As a parent, I would rather have imperfect children who love me and (at times) need me than perfect ones who feel no emotional connection with me at all. If my kids always made the right decisions but never called or expressed a desire to connect, I would not be a happy daddy. Sure, I want them to make wise decisions. And of course I want them to choose paths that lead them to places that enable them to enjoy life. But I want more than that. And so does your heavenly Father. So, instead of sending us a matrix for decision making or a GPS, he's asked us to trust him. To lean on him. To acknowledge his right to rule. And in exchange, he will make our paths clear. Again, divine direction begins with submission. Good information does not guarantee good decision making. And neither does insight or even wisdom.

Ironically, Solomon serves as both a best- and worst-case illustration.

WHERE SOLOMON WENT WRONG

In spite of his great knowledge, unmatched insight, and vast wisdom, there was a time in Solomon's life when he decided to trust in his own understanding. And he paid dearly. In fact, the entire nation paid for that decision to lean on his own flawed understanding. As is typically the case, his flawed logic had to do with his choice in women.

When God established the nation of Israel, he strictly forbade the men to marry foreign women. That included the king. In fact, this command was especially important for the king to obey for a couple of reasons. First, as the king goes, so goes the nation. Second, kings generally married foreigners as a way of ensuring good relations with nearby and oftentimes hostile neighbors. God did not want Israel's leaders leaning into their neighbors for protection. He wanted the nation to rely solely on him.

But in this one area, Solomon opted for the conventional wisdom of the day over obedience and submission to God. So he married Pharaoh's daughter (1 Kings 3). Politically speaking, it was a great move. Israel would never need to worry about going to war with the nation of Egypt. But as strategic as his decision might have been, it was in direct conflict with the command of God. Solomon was declaring his dependency on a foreign king rather than God. In an attempt to ensure peace and avoid bloodshed, Solomon opted for a path that would eventually divide his heart and his loyalties. Ultimately his decision would divide the entire kingdom.

Pharaoh's daughter was just the beginning. Once he aligned himself with Egypt, it must have dawned on him that Egypt's enemies had just become his enemies. Once again, conventional wisdom whispered in his ear, and he listened. Eventually he married women from just about every nation in the region. The writer of 1 Kings described it this way:

> Now King Solomon loved many foreign women along with the daughter of Pharaoh: Moabite, Ammonite, Edomite, Sidonian, and Hittite women, from the nations concerning which the LORD had said to the sons of Israel, "You shall not associate with them, nor shall they associate with you, for they will surely turn your heart away after their gods." Solomon held fast to these in love. He had seven hundred wives, princesses, and three hundred concubines, and his wives turned his heart away. (1 Kings 11:1–3 NASB)

Seven hundred wives! Think about that. Seven hundred mothers-in-law. What was he thinking? Apparently he wasn't. And don't miss the last line of that passage: "*and his wives turned his heart away.*" Away from what? We find the answer to that question in the verses that follow:

> For when Solomon was old, his wives turned his heart away after other gods; and his heart was not wholly devoted to the LORD his God, as the heart of David his father had been. For Solomon went after Ashtoreth the goddess of the Sidonians and after Milcom the detestable idol of the Ammonites. (1 Kings 11:4–5 NASB)

Solomon's decision to prioritize his relationships with foreign kings over his relationship with God cost him his relationship with God. Not because God pulled away but because Solomon's heart was pulled away. A decision designed to protect his nation ultimately corrupted his heart. His heart was turned away from *the* thing God desired most. Relationship. A relationship characterized by dependence and trust. When Solomon opted for what made sense culturally, he leaned away from what made sense relationally. And, in time, his heart was corrupted. Before long he was allowing things that earlier in his administration he would have had people executed for. He actually financed the construction of altars to the pagan gods Chemosh and Molech (1 Kings 11:7). This was unthinkable. Unimaginable. A direct violation of the first commandment. But in his confused state, these decisions made perfect sense to the *wisest man in the world*! Why? Because submission—not talent, information, or insight—is the key to good decision making. Once Solomon abandoned his posture of surrender, he made one bad decision after another. Once again, we see a smart person plagued by bad decisions.

In his attempt to strengthen Israel's relationship with her neighbors, Solomon actually weakened it. Soon after his death, the nation was divided into two weaker kingdoms. For generations these two lesser kingdoms would be plagued by a series of kings who followed Solomon's example of marrying foreign women and adopting their pagan religious practices. Solomon chose a path he sincerely believed would shore up the nation's national security. But the path he chose undermined the nation's dependency on God and ultimately eroded the nation's moral fabric. His decision was not merely a decision. It was a path. And like all paths, this one had a destination.

The moral of the story is this: In order to make the best decisions *now*, we need much more than information, common sense, or conventional wisdom. We need God. We need to live with a posture of dependency. We need to acknowledge him in all our ways. We don't know exactly what motivated Solomon to make such a radical departure from what he knew God asked of him. Was it pride? After all, he *was* the wisest man in the kingdom, and everybody knew it. Was it fear? Did the fact that he ruled the wealthiest kingdom in the region cause him to feel like a target for his neighbors? Perhaps lust? Maybe a combination of all three? We don't know. But what we do learn from this narrative is that apparently *pride*, *fear*, and *lust* all have the potential to override wisdom, discernment, and insight. One or a combination of those three lured the wisest man in the world down a path no one would ever have imagined him traveling. And regardless of his power and experience, he still arrived at the prescribed destination. If the wisdom, understanding, and insight of a man like Solomon does not ensure against choosing the wrong path, isn't it foolish for us to lean on our limited insight and understanding? If Solomon needed something other than his own intuition to protect him from a misguided decision, how about you?

Solomon's story should give each of us reason for concern, because deep in our hearts we all believe that we are too smart to make decisions that will adversely affect our lives. We are convinced that we are too careful. Too shrewd. Too experienced. But that's because our propensity is to *lean* on our own understanding, to trust our own judgment. In spite of Solomon's story, in spite of chapters from our own stories, our natural bent will always be toward trusting in ourselves. We will be inclined to make decisions based on conventional wisdom.

So we each have a choice to make. Will we surrender to the will of our heavenly Father, or will we continue to lean on our own wisdom and insight? Will we acknowledge God in all our ways, or will we pick and choose? I would suggest that you take a few moments to wrestle through three questions. Regardless of your response to the content of this chapter, you owe it to yourself to discover your answers to these questions:

- Why do I hesitate to give God full access to every part of my life?

- What do I fear will happen on the other side of that decision?
- What is the most difficult area of my life to yield control?

Every path has a destination. Direction, not intention, determines destination. Divine direction begins with submission. Information is not enough. Insight is not enough. We need God. And so you are invited to:

> Trust in the LORD with all your heart
>> lean not on your own understanding;
> In all your ways acknowledge him;
>> and he will make your paths straight. (Prov. 3:5–6)

SEVEN

THE STORY
YOU WILL TELL

My dad, like many dads, had a half dozen stories he repeated on a regular basis. When I was young, I often wondered if he *knew* he was repeating himself. Now I realize these stories represented the metanarrative of his life. These were the events that shaped his view of the world and later helped him make sense of the otherwise randomness of life. One of these stories revolved around his early days as a pastor in the mountain community of Fruitland, North Carolina. First Baptist Church Fruitland was a tiny church tucked away in the beautiful Smoky Mountains. On an average Sunday, a couple dozen mountain folks and a few farmers would gather to worship and listen to my dad preach. In addition to pastoring the church, my dad taught in the Bible school right across the street.

The story line that emerged from his years in Fruitland went something like this: "When I showed up in Fruitland, I would work all week to come up with something fresh to say on Sunday morning. I studied. I outlined. I prayed. I would stay up late on Saturday night memorizing and practicing. But after a few weeks, I began to feel like I was wasting my time. When I looked out at those precious mountain people, I found myself thinking, *I don't need to prepare so hard. Most of these folks never finished high school. None of them have been to college. They don't know the difference between a well-crafted, thoroughly researched sermon and a last-minute devotional thought.*

"But every time I was tempted to wing it, every time I considered pulling an outline out of one of those mail-order sermon outline catalogs, I felt like God was saying, 'Charles, don't prepare with just this audience in mind. You prepare for the future. Prepare as if you were speaking to thousands of people, not dozens.' So that's exactly what I did." End of story.

I must have heard that tale a dozen times or so growing up. But I never felt that it had any bearing on my life, until my first year of graduate school. I was twenty-three and had just been asked to teach a college Sunday school class at the church I was attending in Dallas. I was excited. I started preparing on Monday. I worked on my lesson a little bit every night. The Saturday before my debut, I spent almost the entire day preparing. When I showed up for duty Sunday morning, there were about a hundred college students gathered in an assembly area. After a few songs the group would split up and attend one of a dozen or so elective classes, one of which was mine. When the assembly dismissed, I headed down the hall to my classroom, eager to meet my pupils.

I took my place at the marker board and waited. Once everyone had found a seat, there were seven eager faces staring at me. I went out in the hall to see if anyone else was heading my way, but the halls were empty. Everybody had found his or her class.

I was a bit disappointed. But I went ahead and taught my heart out to those seven students. After Sunday school I headed off to big church. As I sat there staring at my hymnal, thinking about the events of the previous hour, I remembered my dad's story. But now it took on significance. I had a decision to make, not unlike the one he had made years before. I smiled to myself and made up my mind then and there to prepare as if I were teaching the entire department rather than a class of seven. I showed up the following weeks with handouts and a portable tape recorder (remember those?). I started recording my lessons on Sunday mornings and listening to them on Sunday nights. I was ridiculously over-prepared. But it didn't matter. I wasn't preparing for the seven. I was preparing for whatever and whomever might be in my future. All that to say, I'm very grateful for my dad's seemingly random story about the early days in Fruitland.

And the point of all that is what?

Solomon Should Have Paid Attention

Like me, King Solomon grew up listening to random stories from his father as well. But unlike the stories most fathers tell, King David's stories were legendary. Songs had been written about his exploits. Everyone knew the story of how David slew the giant from Philistia when he was just a shepherd boy. Goliath's sword had been put on display. David cast a big shadow. Following him as king would be challenging. But as his son, Solomon had a unique advantage. He knew the secret to David's success. His stories of success and failure all pointed back to the same unifying principle—a principle that Solomon himself summarized better than anyone: *trust in the Lord with all your heart.* That was the theme and the lesson from David's life, a lesson Solomon knew and embraced early on, but then drifted from later in life.

One of the legendary stories Solomon grew up hearing revolved around his father and the previous king, Saul. This incident, maybe more than any other, reflected the dilemma that Solomon would one day face himself, when trusting in the Lord and conventional wisdom were in conflict. Here's the story, along with a bit of context.

Following his run-in with Goliath in the valley of Elah, David was immediately catapulted into the limelight. He became famous and influential in the course of a single day. And after marrying the king's daughter, he became wealthy as well. He was a folk hero in every sense of the word. People wrote and sang songs celebrating David's success. The hook went like this: "Saul slew his thousands, and David slew his ten thousands" (1 Sam. 29:5 KJV). In other words, "King Saul is all right, but David is amazing. We used to want to be like Saul. Now we want to be like David."

Now, Saul, being the average king with a giant ego, didn't warm to this turn of events. He didn't appreciate the fact that his popularity among the people was tanking. Complicating matters was this nasty rumor saying the prophet Samuel had visited David's house when he was a lad and had anointed him as the next king of Israel. Such a thing was unheard-of while the reigning king was still . . . reigning. As grateful as Saul was for David's military exploits, he wasn't about to be upstaged by a shepherd boy.

Besides, Saul, like most kings, planned for his son, Jonathan, to follow him to the throne. As long as David was around, if something happened to Saul, Saul knew the people would ignore his son and flock to the shepherd boy to crown him king. Worse still, Jonathan and David had become friends! How could this be? David was the competition.

So Saul decided that the best thing to do was get rid of David.

One day while David was playing his harp for Saul, the king picked up his javelin and threw it with all of his might at David . . . and missed. This happened not once but on two occasions. Apparently David was a slow learner. And fortunately, Saul was a poor marksman.

As a musician, David knew that when the audience began throwing things, it was time to close up shop and look for another gig. So that's exactly what he did. He escaped to the wilderness, where he gathered a group of disenfranchised men around him to serve as his warriors.

And so began a game of cat and mouse that lasted for several years. David would hide in the hills until Saul's spy network found him. Saul would bring on the chase, and David would flee for his life, always staying a step or two ahead of his pursuers. It was during one of these episodes that David was forced to make a decision with consequences that would follow him the rest of his life. He found himself in a situation where the path of conventional wisdom led in one direction and the path that reflected trust in God led somewhere else entirely.

THE DESERT OF ENGEDI

We pick up the story line found in 1 Samuel 24:1. After pursuing the Philistines in battle, Saul and his army returned home and were greeted with great news. David's location had been found—he was hiding in a place called the desert of Engedi. It's not your typical desert with blowing sand dunes. Rather, it's a stretch of land adjacent to the coast of the Dead Sea, where the valley is lush and green, while the mountains are rocky and treacherous.

Picture the scene.

Saul's men had just taken off their battle gear from fighting the Philistines. Their feet ached. Their clothes were caked with sweat, blood, and dirt from who knows how long out on the battlefield. In spite of their success, Saul was ready to turn around and head out again to pursue David. Calling together three thousand of his best warriors, Saul announced that they were moving out.

But Saul was so singularly focused on killing David that he couldn't afford to wait another minute. He had to have David's head. Following orders, his men saddled up their horses while Saul hopped on his mule. At this point, the plot thickens. After a long, forced march, "He came to the sheep pens along the way; a cave was there, and Saul went in to relieve himself" (v. 3). Translation: Saul needed a potty break.

Saul got off of his mule and scanned the terrain for a place to have some royal privacy. Picking a random cave from the many caves in the area, he walked over with a couple of his bodyguards, positioned them at the entrance, and stepped inside to do his business.

But of all the places to stop, and of all the caves to choose, Saul "coincidentally" picked the very cave where David and his men were hiding. Best we can tell, when David got word that Saul was on his trail, he decided to hide his men in the caves and allow Saul and his men to pass through. Once Saul had passed by, David and his men planned to slip out quietly and move in the opposite direction. But nature called. And Saul had to stop.

Saul, completely unaware of his predicament, disrobed and was in the most vulnerable position he could possibly be in. But with his guards posted just outside, what could happen? He felt perfectly safe. Meanwhile, deep in the back recesses of the cavern, David and his men were not believing what they were seeing. This was a miracle. Clearly, God had intervened in their favor.

In terms of the conventional wisdom of the day, killing Saul made perfect sense. Somebody had to go—either Saul or David. It was a simple equation of kill or be killed. Arguably, to kill Saul right then would have been considered an act of self-defense. If they had let Saul live, Saul would have repaid David by continuing to hunt him down.

But this went way beyond conventional wisdom. There was a divine element to the situation. And David's men were quick to point this out. "This is the day of which the LORD said to you, 'Behold, I will deliver your enemy into your hand, that you may do to him as it seems good to you'" (v. 4 NKJV). In so many words, they were telling David, "This is a God thing." I mean, there were signs everywhere. They had heard the story of Samuel anointing David king when he was a teenager. They had heard David speak of God's promise to remove his enemies. By killing Saul, David would be fulfilling two of God's promises. He would both destroy an enemy and become king. The only way for David to be king was for Saul to die. The solution seemed obvious.

From David's men's perspective, there was another compelling reason to kill Saul. His death might very well mean their lives would be spared. The death of this one man would mean less blood spilled later. They lived every day with the reality that it could be their last. A military encounter with Saul and his highly trained men would not bode well for the men closest to David. If David were captured, surely his rebel band would be put to the sword. A decision to spare Saul's life would be a decision to continue to put their lives in jeopardy.

The pressure on David to act was immense. At any second, Saul would finish his business and move on. An opportunity like this was not likely to come again. This was an extraordinarily emotionally charged environment.

THE VALLEY OF DECISION

For a moment, let's leave David in the cave and dig a little deeper into this dynamic. All of life, you see, is filled with decision-making situations that occur in emotionally charged environments. Put another way, *your decision-making environments are not emotionally neutral.* More often than not, the circumstances we face are saturated with powerful emotions. Those emotions easily turn into misguided passions. In the end, passion clouds the ability to accurately evaluate the circumstance in order to choose the right path.

Think about the emotions swirling around your last big purchase—a car, for instance. You promised yourself to buy something used (make that "pre-owned") and practical (such as a four-door sedan), and to pay cash. In spite of your good intentions, your feet took you into the lion's den (I mean, dealer's showroom), where you were captivated by the brand-spanking-new coupe rotating under the bright showroom lights.

That's when your emotions ambushed you.

While your head was rubbernecking in the direction of the main event, the savvy salesman played upon your duly noted emotional pull and ramped up the sales pitch and pressure. "If you buy now, I'm authorized to make you a deal that's really not a whole lot more than what you were looking at outside." Before you knew it, you were driving away in a new car with seventy-two months of payments.

Or think about relational decisions you've made. There are no emotionally neutral relationships. It is almost impossible to gain or maintain objectivity when making relational decisions. Emotions cloud our ability to see things as they actually are. Consequently, once the fog lifts, we wonder why what is so painfully clear now was so hidden then. But that's the nature of relationships.

Emotionally driven decision making rarely leads us down the right path. In the emotion of the moment, we are easily swayed by conventional wisdom, cultural norms, the herd mentality, or even our own patterns of behavior. Patterns that didn't serve us well in the past but are so familiar we just trek that way out of habit. These are the paths of least resistance. So we opt for them. Emotionally charged decision-making environments make it almost impossible to gain the perspective we need to choose paths that take us where we want to go. That's why David's story is so remarkable.

Driven by the emotions swirling around that cave, and drawing upon the time-tested, conventional wisdom any warrior would know from firsthand experience, David knew killing Saul was the thing to do. It's no wonder all of his advisors were lobbying for a quick end to this tiresome game. What kind of leader would hesitate when his enemy's head was delivered to him on a platter?

And there was yet another component fueling David's emotionally charged decision-making environment: a moral imperative. What's that? A moral imperative is any situation in which there's a wrong that needs to be righted. For David, the moral imperative had to do with Saul's behavior as king. Clearly, Saul demonstrated by the way he governed that he wasn't interested in listening to the voice of God through the prophet Samuel. As a result, Saul brought grief, suffering, and unnecessary death to Israel.

That had to be stopped.

And now the stars had aligned. His moment had come. David went into the cave a fugitive, but he would emerge as king. The momentum was in his favor. God had spoken. The king must die.

But remarkably, David displayed restraint—restraint that made absolutely no sense to his men at the time. Somehow David was able to resist the momentum of the circumstances and choose a different course of action.

David saw something the men around him did not see. He had a sense of clarity they lacked, clarity that sliced through the fog of emotion. Clarity that enabled him to resist the pressure to choose a course of action he would someday regret. What did he see that no one else was able to see? That became evident in the events and conversation that followed.

DAVID'S DECISION

In 1 Samuel 24:4 we read, "Then David crept up unnoticed and cut off a corner of Saul's robe." Why? We're not told. Meanwhile, David's men were watching him sneak up on Saul's position, assuming an assassination was about to take place. They were already picturing themselves on David's left and right hand during his coronation. When David returned to his men with a piece of Saul's robe, they were confused and disappointed to say the least. To complicate things even further, David informed his men that he felt guilty for what he did (v. 5). And of course they thought, *Huh? So, you didn't kill Saul, and now you're bothered by taking a swatch of fabric? Are you going soft on us, David? Are we missing something here? What's your problem? You just let Saul slip through your hands! Our hands!*

At this point David explained why he would not take Saul's life. There were three things that argued against it. Two are obvious from what David said to his men. The third one is implied. Specifically:

1. The law of God
2. The principles of God
3. The wisdom of God

Here's David's response to his men's disappointment: "The LORD forbid that I should do anything to my master" (v. 6). In other words, "Guys, in case you've forgotten, Saul is still the king. And unless something has changed, *it's against the law to kill the king*." Now, there's a thought. This wasn't something David needed to pray about; God had already addressed it. You don't kill or murder or dishonor the king. Period. By cutting off a piece of his robe, David had symbolically attacked Saul. So he felt guilty. A feeling not shared among his men.

Listen to what comes next. "The LORD forbid that I should do such a thing to my master, the LORD's anointed, or lift my hand against him; for he is the anointed of the LORD." Here David pointed to a principle he knew he had no business violating. Simply put, he had no right to *replace* what God had put *in* place. Since God chose to make Saul king, David had no right to remove him as king. This was God's decision to make, not David's. Regardless of Saul's actions, he was still God's choice as king. And David would honor that. David had confidence that the same God who put Saul in place could handle taking him out of that place without David's meddling. What's more, to displace what God had put in place would make David an enemy of God.

As Saul was gathering his things and preparing to leave the cave, the scripture tells us that "David rebuked his men and did not allow them to attack Saul. And Saul left the cave and went his way" (v. 7).

By refusing to kill Saul, David kept God's law and applied an important principle. But David's decision incorporated a third component as well: refusing to kill Saul was actually the *wise* thing to do. That became evident through what happened next.

David gave Saul time to dress, return to his army, and saddle up his donkey. Once David knew it was safe, he made his move. Leaving his men in the dark, David walked to the mouth of the cave and announced his presence. Saul and his men were stunned as David emerged, prostrating himself face down on the ground. Everyone in Saul's entourage understood the implications of David's presence in the cave. Saul was lucky to be alive. His guards had failed to guard him. Then David broke the tension by calling out:

> "My lord the king! . . . Why do you listen when men say, 'David is bent on harming you'? This day you have seen with your own eyes how the LORD delivered you into my hands in the cave. Some urged me to kill you, but I spared you; I said, 'I will not lift my hand against my master because he is the LORD's anointed.'" (vv. 8–10)

Still in shock at what had almost happened, Saul and his men listened as David threw one last punch. In verse 12, David says, "May the LORD judge between you and me. And may the LORD avenge the wrongs you have done to me, but my hand will not touch you." Put another way, "Saul, you deserve to die for all you've done to me. You don't deserve to be king, but I'm going to leave that in the Lord's hands rather than take matters into my own."

Imagine the drama of that moment. Imagine the tension in the air. Clearly, David was the better man. He had behaved more like a king than the king by refusing to break God's law and abiding by God's principles. And in his closing remarks, David tipped us off to a third dynamic that drove his decision to spare Saul's life. Sparing Saul was actually the wise thing to do.

David knew that the events of that day would eventually become a story that would be told and retold, possibly for generations. The events of that day would be part of his legacy. What story would he want told? Would he want his rise to power to be predicated upon his surprise attack on a vulnerable king in a cave? Was that how he wanted his ascension to the throne to begin? Besides, men who stole a throne through bloodshed often lost it the same way. You live by the sword, you die by the sword. To assassinate Saul would have been a foolish move, one that would have marred his reputation for the rest of his life. To kill the king would have been a declaration of his dependency on his own cunning rather than on the protection and provision of God. He would have declared himself judge and jury.

Fortunately, David was able to see all of that in spite of the emotion of the moment. In spite of his companions' advice. In spite of his own fear. In refusing to kill Saul, he modeled a powerful truth: *one never accomplishes the will of God by breaking the law of God, violating the principles of God, or ignoring the wisdom of God.*

FINDING CLARITY

Every big decision you make will have an emotional component to it, whether it is purchasing a home, choosing an academic major, or deciding when to start a family. Every big decision takes you down a path; it impacts your future in some way. Life is too short to allow the emotions of the moment to move you in a direction you will later regret. You need a strategy to help you cut through the emotional fog that clouds most decision-making environments.

I'm convinced David's story presents us with just such a plan. By adhering to the law, principles, and the wisdom of God, David was able to overcome the inertia that was sweeping him down a path he would wish he had never taken. By paying attention to these three things, David saw through the fallacy of conventional wisdom (kill the king to be the king). He didn't get caught up in the idea that by killing the king he would be saving lives. The law, principles, and the wisdom of God provided him with the clarity he needed to do the right thing the right way at the right time, in spite of incredible pressure to do otherwise.

So I want to encourage you to apply these three questions to every option that comes your way:

1. Does this option violate God's law?

2. Does this option violate a principle?

3. In light of the story I want to tell, what is the wise thing to do?

If, while in the throes of decision making, you pause and temporarily detach yourself from the emotion and the urgency of the moment and ask these three questions, you will gain extraordinary clarity. They will enable you to see each option in a new light.

Another way of asking the first question is, *Has God already spoken on this matter?*

In the Scriptures we are confronted with God's laws regarding just about every situation imaginable. From marriage, money, sex, authority, parenting, you name it. There are dozens of issues that God has made his will clear about. Twice in my life I've had married men tell me they were praying about whether they should leave their wives for their girlfriends or end the relationship with their girlfriends and recommit to their marriages. In both instances I assured these men that they really didn't need to pray any further; God had already covered that one. In contrast to the powerful emotions that clouded their thinking, the path they were to take was already spelled out. God's will was actually very clear.

However, the second question is more difficult, because the principles of God are not as obvious as the law of God. They are often built around a cause-and-effect relationship. To discover if the options you are considering violate a principle, ask yourself, *What outcome am I expecting from this decision? Does the option I'm considering naturally lead to that outcome?*

In emotionally charged decision-making environments, we often assume cause-and-effect relationships that don't really exist. For example, purchasing is often an attempt to satisfy a craving.

But consumption doesn't lead to contentment. In the moment it feels like it will, but when you push past the emotion and ask, *What outcome do I desire?* and *Will this option get me there?* the answers become painfully clear. In the same way, debt doesn't lead to happiness. So when we make a happiness purchase that requires debt, we violate a principle. We assume a connection or relationship that doesn't really exist.

Another way to ask the third question, the wisdom question, is to ask, *What story do I want to tell?* As was the case with David, some decisions are legacy decisions. To some degree, every decision becomes part of your story. In light of the story you want to tell, what should you do? David decided that killing the king while he was relieving himself was not the story he wanted to tell his grandkids one day. Imagine that scenario: "Granddaddy, please tell us one more time the story of how you snuck up behind king Saul and ran him through with your spear while he was on the potty. You are such a mighty warrior."

Whatever the issue, as you consider your options, consider what you will say about it. When you look back on this chapter of your life, what is the story you will want to tell? A story of being swept away by the emotion of the moment? A story of how you allowed conventional wisdom to drive you down a path that you later regretted? Perhaps a story of following cultural norms? A story where you were just part of the herd? Probably not.

If you will pause and consider the three questions I've suggested, your story will be quite different. Your story will be more like David's: a story showing that in the midst of powerful emotion, you gained clarity and did the unusual thing, the thing that set you apart from the herd. A story you will be proud of. A story you won't mind repeating.

IN THE END

In this instance David honored the law, principles, and wisdom of God, and the story ended well. Not initially, but eventually. Seven chapters later we find Saul battling the Philistines. Israel was losing ground. Saul's bodyguards closed in around him to protect him from the onslaught of the enemy. But in spite of their valiant efforts, a random Philistine archer drew his bow and shot an arrow in the direction of Saul and his inner circle of warriors. It pierced Saul's armor and mortally wounded him. Afraid that the Philistines would make sport of him, Saul fell on his sword and ended his own life. So he died on the battlefield. Soon after Saul's death, David was proclaimed king, just as God had promised. I've got to believe David breathed a sigh of relief every time he thought about how close he'd come to assassinating King Saul.

LAW, PRINCIPLES, WISDOM

God's will for your life will always line up with his law, his principles, and his wisdom. As we said earlier in this chapter, one never accomplishes the will of God by breaking the law of God, violating the principles of God, or ignoring the wisdom of God.

When you bring these three things to bear on the options you face, you will gain clarity in even the most emotionally charged circumstances, just as David did. And if you are willing to act on what you discover, you will have a story to tell—a story you can be proud of. Perhaps it will become one of those stories you repeat over and over for someone coming along behind you. And maybe, like my dad's story, like David's story, God will use it to bring clarity to someone who is in the process of creating a story of his or her own.

EIGHT

A Little Help from Our Friends

Remember maps? You know, the old paper version of a GPS? Remember maps before MapQuest and Google Maps? I can remember being a kid on vacation with my family and watching my mom unfold a map of Florida that was almost as large as the state itself. I remember my dad swatting at it like it was some kind of creature intent on blocking his view of the road. And no one, including the manufacturer, could actually refold those things back to their original size. The goal, of course, was to refold it so that the panel that said *State of Florida* was on the outside. But that never happened. So eventually we had a glove compartment full of mystery maps. They were only used once because nobody had the patience to unfold one of those babies only to discover that it was the wrong one.

There will always be a need for maps or their equivalent. From time to time we will all need outside assistance getting from where we are to where we want or need to be. Nobody has the time or patience to meander through a neighborhood, looking for a street or a specific address. Once we venture beyond our regular stomping grounds, we need assistance. We need a map.

The same is true in life. We are all trying to get somewhere we've never been before. And none of us has time to meander around trying to find our way. The seasons of our lives pass quickly, and we don't get to redo any of them. Life is a series of one-and-onlies, firsts-and-lasts. The problem, of course, is that there is no MapQuest for life. Imagine what that would look like.

Starting location: single with several bad habits
Ending location: happily married

Starting location: school loans, credit card debt, no budget
Ending location: debt-free, with money to burn

Or how about,

Starting location: two lazy, out-of-control kids
Ending location: two premed students with full rides

Obviously, that kind of outside help is not available. Not that I'm aware of, anyway. But whereas there isn't a Web site that provides that kind of direction, there are people who know how to get to those places. We know that because we've seen 'em there, haven't we? We know some people who have the kind of marriage we long for. We've met people whose financial house seems to be in order. No doubt you've run into people who are able to maintain healthy relationships instead of bumping around from person to person. You know couples with kids who are a joy to be around. Regardless of where it is you want to go, others have been there and done that. And guess what? They probably know how they got there. They have a map. And you would do well to take a peek at it if you get the opportunity.

RIGHT MAPS, WRONG MAPS

Now, as obvious as all of that may sound, I am constantly amazed at how resistant folks are to take their cues from people who are where they want to be. But I'm even more amazed at how quick the average person is to borrow a page or two from the map of someone who's never been where he wants to be. How about the parents who parent like their parents and wonder why their kids are turning out the same way they did? And then there are the couples who treat each other the way they saw their moms and dads treat each other and wonder why they are just as unhappy as their parents were. These are folks who have a good idea of where they want to be but are content to follow a map used by folks who've never been there.

This happens all the time among friends. The great thing about having friends who share your season of life is that you have so much in common. But the downside to that is they aren't much farther down the road of life than you are. Friends are great for friendship. They aren't always that great for advice giving. And often it is not their advice that gets us into trouble—it is the assumptions we make based on what we observe about our friends. These assumptions become a map we inadvertently follow. I call this phenomenon the *herd assumption*. The herd assumption happens when you *assume* that since everybody you know is doing something the same way, it must be all right. If everybody you know is mortgaged to the hilt, driving two leased vehicles, and applying for a home equity line of credit, then it can't be all that bad. If everybody you know is sleeping with whomever they happen to be dating at the time, then that's just the way the world works. If everybody you know works sixty hours a week and sees their family primarily on weekends, then it must work out. Somehow. The problem, of course, is that everybody is headed for a similar destination at which no one has yet arrived. It *feels* safe. Everyone can't be wrong.

But it's not safe. And by the time it becomes obvious that each of those three directions leads to undesirable destinations, it is usually too late to do much about it.

Taking your cues from people who share your season of life is the equivalent of asking for and following the directions of someone who's never been where you want to go. And in some cases it is much worse than that. It may be like taking directions from someone who is lost! You would never do that in a driving context. But you may be doing that right now in arenas that have far greater implications for your future than wasting a few hours driving in circles. The maps your friends are following may be unreliable. And life is too short to wait and see.

ALL SKATE

All of us take our cues in life from someone. Even you. Right now, at this very moment, your financial, relational, moral, spiritual, and professional decisions are being impacted, perhaps dictated, by the patterns or paths of other people. You are taking your cues from someone. By that I don't mean decisions regarding the daily details of your life. I'm referring to the general patterns you are following. Since that is the case, you would do well to stop and reflect upon where you got your life maps to begin with. Did you consciously choose them? Did you inherit them? Did you pick up a set of maps as a reaction to the way you were raised? Are you just moving with the herd? Did you seek out advice from someone older and wiser? Whose maps are you borrowing from? Whose pattern are you following? Whose journey are you emulating? One of the most crucial decisions you will make is the decision regarding whose map you are going to follow.

If your response to those questions is, "I'm not following anybody's maps! I am my own person!" then you need to know that you are following the pattern or map of all those people in the world who consider themselves unconventional individualists. And there are lots of 'em, which means they are really not all that individual or unconventional. But don't tell them. Choosing to live contrary to what's considered *conventional* is a well-worn path. It leads somewhere. My point isn't that it leads somewhere bad. It's just that you should know *unconventional* is a path. You are, in fact, taking your cues from someone. And if you will admit that, you will be able to leverage that knowledge for your own benefit. Here's how.

Turn Left Here

Since we are all taking our cues from someone, somewhere—consciously or unconsciously—we would do well to be a bit more intentional about whom we borrow from. Imagine the dead-ends and regrets we could avoid if we took our cues from the right people. What if, instead of relying on the advice and example of people who are no farther down the road than you are, you started soliciting travel advice from people who've been to or perhaps live where it is you want to go? Imagine how much better your decision making would be if you decided to ignore the advice and resist the lifestyles of those who are apparently lost anyway, and began taking your cues from individuals and couples who are where you want to be? I'm not suggesting you try to become someone other than who God made you to be. I *am* suggesting that in the core arenas of life—finances, family, morality, spirituality, friendship, profession, education—we all have a mental picture of how we want things to turn out. So why wouldn't we want to learn what we can from people whose lives and lifestyles reflect our goals and aspirations? Why in the world would we take our cues from anyone else?

People Who Know

Here's something I've observed about successful people (and in this instance you can define success any way you want). Successful people, people who are where you want to be, are willing to acknowledge what they don't know. And they are not too proud to borrow from the maps of people who do know. We perceive successful people as individuals who have all the answers and who don't need anyone to tell them what to do. So we assume that's how they got to where they are. Not true. While it is true that some people quit listening once they become successful, that is not how they got there to begin with.

Successful people are often credited with being smart. And many are. But the successful people I know don't attribute their success to their IQs. They attribute it to the collective wisdom and insight they garnered from others. Successful people aren't successful because they knew everything they needed to know. They are successful because they were willing to apply the lessons they learned from others. Are there exceptions? Of course there are. But planning to be an exception is not much of a plan. Planning to be *lucky* is no plan at all. I know a guy who survived a head-on collision and he wasn't wearing a seat belt. He was lucky. He was an exception. But I think I'll continue to wear a seat belt.

Successful people, whether in the arena of family, marriage, business, finances, or ministry, know their limits. They understand the value of time. They know when they have ventured beyond the realm of their expertise and experience. They know when it is time to borrow a page out of someone else's playbook. One the best things you can do is reject the notion that because people expect you to have all the answers, you must therefore pretend that you do. Being a parent does not mean you know how to be a great parent. Being a husband or wife is not the equivalent of knowing how to have a great marriage. Having a position of responsibility does not ensure that you know everything you need to know to handle that responsibility responsibly. Position does not equal ability. The moment you say, "I do" or have that first child or open that first checking account or start that new business or begin that new relationship is like venturing into a part of town that you are totally unfamiliar with. The ability to drive does not equal the ability to navigate. You need outside assistance. But you need the *right* outside assistance.

PULLING OVER

Successful people know when they're in over their heads. They don't deceive themselves or others; they don't act like they're smarter than they are. They know when they've reached their limits: the end of their knowledge, too much emotion, an inadequate amount of information. They understand that reaching a destination requires learning to recognize when they are in no condition to decide what their next move should be.

It takes a lot of security to say, "Even though I'm in charge, I have no idea what to do on this issue." "I'm your father, but I don't know the answer to that." "I'm your mother, but we need to think about this." "I'm the head of this company, but I'm just not sure what plan of action to follow."

With all of that in mind, we should not be shocked to discover that one of the primary avenues through which God directs us is the counsel of others. And that applies whether we're in a time-critical situation where a decision must be made quickly, an emotionally charged situation where we can't see straight, or in scenarios where we're simply out of our league and incapable of choosing the right course.

SOLOMON SAYS

As we've seen throughout this book, the wisest person who ever lived (other than Jesus) was King Solomon. God gave him a supernatural gift of wisdom and promised that he would be wiser than any other mortal before or since. Consequently, Solomon was architect, poet, philosopher, scientist, scholar, theologian, and ruler extraordinaire. He was the go-to guy for everything. And yet he had more to say about seeking the wisdom and direction of others than any other biblical author. Think about that. The wisest man who ever lived insists that we need outside assistance.

Now, why would he have so much to say on this topic? After all, he was already the wisest man in the world—he didn't need any counsel. And to top it off, he was a king. Kings are not known for their reliance on others or their willingness to listen. Nonetheless, he put a high premium on getting advice or direction from others. According to Solomon, wise people listen and learn.

Here's a sampling of Solomon's advice on advice from others.

A wise man will hear and increase in learning,

And a man of understanding will acquire wise counsel.

(Prov. 1:5 NASB)

The way of a fool is right in his own eyes

But a wise man is he who listens to counsel. (12:15 NASB)

Through insolence comes nothing but strife,

But wisdom is with those who receive counsel. (13:10 NASB)

Listen to counsel and accept discipline,
    That you may be wise the rest of your days. (19:20 NASB)

Where there is no guidance the people fall,
    But in abundance of counselors there is victory. (11:14 NASB)

Without consultation, plans are frustrated,
    But with many counselors they succeed. (15:22 NASB)

That's some pretty straightforward advice, isn't it? Wise people listen and prosper. Fools don't, and don't. It is the fool who says what we have all said at some point in our lives: "I don't need anyone to tell me what to do." Chances are, you would have avoided what turned into your greatest regret if you had sought out and listened to wise counsel. There are some destinations you could have avoided if you had stopped and asked for direction. According to Solomon, no one ever gets to the place where he is so smart and experienced that he no longer needs outside input. The wise are always listening. That's how they became wise. That's how they remain wise.

When it comes to seeking outside advice, I'm a fanatic. In fact, the older (and hopefully wiser) I get, the more energized I've become about listening to those who are farther down the road than I am. I learned a long time ago that there is something more important than being right, and that is making the right decision. People who always have to be *right* will always be limited in their decision-making ability. They will be limited to what they know and what they have experienced. And sometimes that is enough. But sometimes it isn't. So why risk it? Why not just decide ahead of time to lean on the knowledge and experience of those who are farther down the road or who have actually arrived at the destination you seek?

One thing that makes it easy for me to listen to outside advice is my experience in ministry. Every week I'm confronted with stories of relational and financial tragedy. And when it is appropriate, I always ask, "Did you consult with anyone before you . . . ? Did you talk to anyone who had faced a similar situation?" Most of the time the response is, "No." Sometimes I get, "No, but I prayed." I'm all for prayer. I'm sure that comes as a shock. But I always suggest that people pray for wisdom and then seek outside assistance. After all, if Solomon is right, wisdom involves stopping to ask for directions. Think about it. If you were driving and got lost, you wouldn't *just* pray. You might pray to find someone who could help you get unlost. But I doubt you would opt for prayer to the exclusion of asking for help. As I've said throughout this chapter, there is far more at stake in the life decisions you make than there is in your driving decisions. If you are willing to ask for directions when you can't find a movie theater, why would you hesitate to ask for input when you are making a big relationship or financial decision?

Then, of course, there are the success stories. I've seen people take good counsel and run with it. I've seen individuals and couples run with it even when it went directly against everything they felt like doing or felt led to do. I've seen couples dig their way out of debt. I've watched as singles broke off engagements. I've seen individuals walk away from once-in-a-lifetime job opportunities. And

I've been doing this long enough to have many of these brave individuals come back around years later and share their gratitude for what at the time was very inconvenient advice. They are in good places now. Enviable places. And by their own admission they didn't get there on their own. They had to lean hard into the counsel and advice of those who were farther down the road.

BE SELECTIVE

Coincidentally, this subject is best illustrated by an event that took place in the life of the young Israelite king Rehoboam. I say *coincidentally* because Rehoboam was Solomon's son, the son Solomon chose to follow him as king. In spite of Solomon's clarity around the idea of seeking wise counsel, Rehoboam was slow to embrace his father's counsel. Being a son and having a couple of sons, I understand the difficulty of listening to dear ol' dad. I bet you do too. My dad was rarely wrong, but it took me a while to figure that out. Anyway, in the Old Testament book of 1 Kings, we are introduced to the heir apparent, Rehoboam.

Here's some background. Solomon had died. The assumption among the people of Israel was that his son Rehoboam would be crowned king. When he showed up in Shechem to be crowned, he was approached by a fellow named Jeroboam, who had been appointed by a group of disgruntled people to go to the new king on their behalf. Their complaint went as follows: "Your father [Solomon] put a heavy yoke on us, but now lighten the harsh labor and the heavy yoke he put on us, and we will serve you" (1 Kings 12:4).

Solomon's aggressive building campaign had placed a heavy burden on the average citizen, especially in that part of the country. Taxes were high. People had been forced to work like slaves. The workload made it almost impossible for them to tend to their own land and herds. With the passing of King Solomon, they were hoping for a reprieve from the endless construction. So they promised his son their devotion if only he would show mercy.

After hearing their request, Rehoboam made two very smart decisions. He asked for time to decide what to do. He was wise enough to know that this was not a time for a rushed decision. So essentially what he told them was, "Come back in three days, and I'll give you my answer."

The second thing he did was seek assistance in making this decision. He chose to listen before he decided. So far, so good. His dad would have been proud. So Rehoboam went to a group of his father's counselors for advice. These were men who had the perspective that only years and experience could provide. They had seen the changes that had taken place in Israel during the reign of Solomon. So they had context for the complaints of the people. The other thing this group had going for them was that because of their tenure, they had little to gain or lose by telling Rehoboam the truth. Here is the advice they gave: "If today you will be a servant to these people and serve them and give them a favorable answer, they will always be your servants" (v. 7). In other words, "Lighten their load!" That was good advice.

But apparently Rehoboam wasn't looking for good advice. He was looking for affirmation. He was looking for someone to tell him what he wanted to hear, someone who would go along with what he had already decided to do. So, the Bible says, "Rehoboam rejected the advice the elders gave him and consulted the young men who had grown up with him and were serving him" (v. 8). He turned to his peers for advice. He turned to a group that was no farther down the path than he was. In fact, they weren't as far down the path as he was—they worked for him. And so they told him exactly what they knew he wanted to hear.

> The young men who had grown up with him replied, "Tell these people who have said to you, 'Your father put a heavy yoke on us, but make our yoke lighter'—tell them, 'My little finger is thicker than my father's waist. My father laid on you a heavy yoke; I will make it even heavier. My father scourged you with whips; I will scourge you with scorpions.'" (vv. 10–11)

That was the advice he wanted to hear. That was the advice he took. Three days later, when Jeroboam and his contingency returned for their answer, Rehoboam assured them that not only was he not going to lighten their load, but he would increase it. Little did he know that he wasn't simply making a decision. He was choosing a path. A path for the entire nation. A path with a destination he could not foresee, but one his father's counselors had. After hearing his decision, the majority of Israel rejected Rehoboam as king. They threw their support behind their spokesman, Jeroboam, and eventually elected him as their king. When Rehoboam sent Adoniram, his chief of forced labor, to round up workers, the people stoned him to death. The two factions went to war, and the nation was divided. All because a young king refused to lean on the advice of those who were farther down the road.

There are many lessons that can be learned from the plight of young king Rehoboam. But perhaps the most important takeaway is this: It is next to impossible to hear the voice of wisdom if we are not really listening for it to begin with. The best counsel in the world is wasted counsel if our minds are already made up.

WHY IS THIS SO DIFFICULT?

Why is it that something so obvious is so difficult? Why would we hesitate to seek counsel? And why would we hesitate to embrace it once we've received it? Perhaps it is the same reason men are slow to pull over and ask for help when driving. Perhaps it is the same reason that when I realize I'm lost, I speed up! Basically, I don't want to be told what to do. And I certainly don't want to discover that I'm wrong. In a word, pride. Pride is hard to see in the bathroom mirror. But it is awfully easy to see in the rearview mirror. Looking back, it is all too clear to me why I refused to listen to the voices of reason when I was in over my head. It was pride. You may label it differently. High-strung. Independent. Type A. Regardless of how you camouflage it, anyone who knows he doesn't know but won't go to those who do know has a problem. And anyone who thinks she knows but won't listen to those in a position to *really* know has an issue as well. And in the end, it is not our advisers and counselors who pay. It is those of us who are too proud to listen. It is not the wise people around us who will find themselves in places they never wanted to be. It's us! The ones who didn't know but drove on like we did anyway.

Mind Your Own

One response I sometimes get when I encourage people to seek a second opinion is, "Well, what I do with my life is really nobody else's business." On the surface that's a bit difficult to argue with. But the fact is, all of our decisions eventually become other people's business. To hide behind that line is very shortsighted. Very. Think about it. Do you know people who made really bad choices regarding whom they married? You do! How do you know? It was none of your business whom they married. But you know, don't you? And you know it was a bad decision. Just about every decision we make becomes other people's business. As soon as a decision becomes public, it becomes everybody's business. You decided privately and independently to buy a house or car or to take a different job—but before you know it, everyone knows where you live and what you drive and where you work. And they also know if those were good decisions or not. I have two friends who, in the privacy of their marriages, decided to purchase new homes before selling the ones they were living in. It was their decision, their money, their future. So why invite anyone else into the decision-making process? And now everybody they know knows they are each stuck with two homes less than six miles from each other. And everybody they know talks about it. One couple has both homes for sale. Everybody they know knows that as well. And just about everybody who knows about their situation would have told 'em it was a bad idea to buy before they sold. But it wasn't really any of our business.

Truth is, not only do our private decisions become known by the public, but they are judged by the public as well. You should know, because you do it all the time. You don't just *discover* what your friends have decided to do—you talk about it and form an opinion. It's just human nature. "I can't believe she's marrying that guy." "Why are they sending their kids to *that* school?" "Doesn't he realize that new job's only a dead end?" Let's be honest—it's true, isn't it? At every level, we pass judgment on the decisions people around us make. But it goes deeper than that.

The decisions we make privately and independently are not only known by others and judged by others, but they also *affect* other people as well. Because I'm a pastor, every decision I make about our church affects a lot of people. I can decide on my own, without consulting anyone, but the effects of my decisions go way beyond me. My decisions as a father can be made privately and independently, but the effects are felt immediately and often profoundly by at least four other people. That's why the teenager who says, "It's my life; leave me alone. I'll do whatever I want" is so deceived. It's why every husband and father or wife and mother who says, "It's my life; don't cramp my style" is so tragically mistaken. At the end of the day, when you finally reap the results of your misguided (or unguided) decisions, you're not the only one who suffers. Every decision we make that hurts us also hurts the people who love us most. And those who depend on us most will be hurt the most.

If the results of our decisions will eventually be seen, judged, and felt by others, why not involve others to begin with? Since nothing remains a secret, why make decisions in secret? Since the people around you who are older and wiser and who are where you someday want to be are going to know what you decided, why not borrow from their experience when making the decision? Since people are going to talk *about* you, why not give some of them an opportunity to talk *to* you before you choose your path?

Here's a fascinating thing. When we make bad choices—choose bad paths—and we realize our mistakes, who do we go to for advice about how to make a course correction? Who do we go to for advice about how to dig out of the hole we dug ourselves into? Answer: the same people who would have steered us in a different direction had we gone to them before we made our decision. If direction determines destination, we would be wise to take some direction before choosing one.

Two Things to Ponder

As we close our discussion on the wisdom of borrowing from other people's maps, I want to leave you with two things to consider. First, *no one gets to the place where he no longer needs wise counsel.* Nobody. To live as if you don't is to deceive yourself. The older we get, the higher the stakes are for many of our decisions. The older we get, the less likely it is that anyone is going to give us advice. Solomon's story ends tragically. Being the wisest man in the world did not shelter him from making unwise decisions. He didn't take his own advice. And apparently no one was in a position to offer him any. We never outgrow the need for the objectivity an outsider can bring. Success, age, wealth, and power do not necessarily translate into wisdom, self-control, or maturity. Besides, success of all types is intoxicating. And intoxicated individuals are not the best decision makers. So remain open to the input of outsiders. And when you can, seek it out.

Second, *you will never reach your full potential without tapping into the wisdom of others.* You just won't. You know what you know. That's all you know. You've experienced what you've experienced. That is the sum total of your experience. Those are two limitations that set you up for poor decision making in areas outside the realm of your knowledge and experience. But learning to learn from those who are ahead of you removes both of those limitations. Your knowledge, insight, and experience may put you miles ahead of the average person. But even then, you won't reach your full potential apart from tapping into the knowledge, insight, and experience of those who are a step ahead of you. The best example of this comes from the world of athletics. Tiger Woods and Michael Phelps both have coaches. And I bet they would have both done pretty well in their respective fields without one. But neither would have accomplished what they have accomplished without the input of their coaches. Borrow from others.

Pull Over

At the beginning of this chapter, I made the statement that all of us are borrowing from someone's map. Sometimes intentionally. Sometimes unintentionally. So whose map are you borrowing from? Who are the influences in your life? Peers? Family? Business associates? Are they any farther down the road than you are? Do their lives and lifestyles reflect your vision for your future? Whose map would you be wise to borrow from? Whom do you know who is where you want to be in her marriage? Whom do you know who seems to have done a good job managing his finances? Who has a family life that reflects where you would like your family to be someday? What can you do to gain a better understanding of how they arrived where they are?

I have a friend who was so committed to finding out what made successful people successful that he offered to pay the people he admired most a hundred dollars for an hour of their time. He told me that no one turned him down and no one took the money. Extreme? Maybe. But what's your future worth? What are your future relationships worth? If a hundred bucks will buy you a peek at the map of someone who is where you want to be someday, that may be the best hundred dollars you ever spend.

No matter where you are—if you are beginning your journey and realize you don't know the way . . . if you are in the middle of the drive but can't see the road ahead because the emotional fog is so thick . . . if you are stopped in your tracks because the terrain is unfamiliar—here's what you need to do: Don't fake it. Don't pretend that you've got it all under control. Pull over and ask for direction. Direction determines destination. Find somebody who knows the way—and heed his advice. Asking doesn't mean you lack wisdom—it's *evidence* of wisdom. Because successful people know what they don't know, and they are quick to go to people who do.

NINE

ATTENTION RETENTION

I don't remember too much about driver's ed. I'm sure it was beneficial, somehow. I think I've parallel parked a grand total of five times since I was sixteen, and that includes the day I went to get my license. So of course I'm extremely grateful for the entire afternoon we devoted to developing that critical skill. I wonder—has anyone ever been injured due to someone's inability to parallel park? The only real damage I can think of related to someone's inability to park on a curb is tire damage. I'm surprised Michelin or Goodyear hasn't lobbied to have parallel parking removed from the driving test. Besides, why should we have to demonstrate our *parking* skills during a *driving* test? But I'm not bitter.

There is one valuable lesson I took away from my two days of driving around with Mr. . . . Mr. . . . I'm sure he's forgotten my name too. The one thing he said that I've applied not only to driving but to many arenas of life is, "Don't look at the cars that are passing you, and don't look at the cars you are passing. If you look that way, you'll tend to steer that way as well." He was right. I have a tendency to drift in the direction of the things that have my attention.

Speaking of attention, if you've been paying attention, you've noticed that this entire book is written around the premise that our direction, not our intention, determines our destination. As we close in on the end of our time together, I want to add one more component to that equation. Like much of the content in this book, this is so obvious that you may wonder why I bother to point it out. But the obvious things are often the things that escape our notice. I'm sure you've visited a friend's home and wondered why she had *that* couch or chair in the living room. It is obvious to everybody who visits. But not to the folks who live there. So bear with me as I draw your attention to something that is obvious as well as overlooked.

What gets our attention determines our direction and, ultimately, our destination. Or if you would prefer the short version: *attention* determines *direction.*

Like my driver's ed teacher warned me, we have a tendency to steer toward the things that have our attention. The things we give our attention to in life influence the direction of our lives. Now, if that's all there was to this, I could conclude this chapter now by giving you some pithy advice like, *So keep your eyes on the road of life, and everything will be fine.* And everything *would* be fine if there weren't any distractions along the road of life. But there are.

ATTENTION GRABBERS

Think about the following sentences: "As soon as I walked in, it grabbed my attention." Or "When she walked into the room, she captured my attention." Have you ever had something or someone *grab* or *capture* your attention? Think about the terms we use to describe this phenomenon: *Grab. Capture.* There is a lot of emotion associated with those two terms. And understandably so. If you have ever had anything *grab* your attention, there was probably a good bit of emotion associated with that moment. You may be driving something that *grabbed* your attention. You may be living in something that *grabbed* your attention. And you may be living with someone who *grabbed*, or maybe it would be better to say *captured*, your attention. I am.

The reason you are driving, living in, or living with something or someone who grabbed your attention is that once it or they had your attention, you drifted in their direction. That's understandable because *attention determines direction*. And that's not always a bad thing.

After finishing graduate school in Dallas, I moved back to Atlanta to find my place in this world (i.e., look for a job). I had hoped my place in this world was the PhD program at Baylor University, but apparently the administration thought somebody else should have my place. So I went home, moved back in with my parents, and went to work for my dad. Not too long after that, a friend of mine invited me to fill in at a Bible study on the Georgia Tech campus. I agreed, showed up on the appointed night, did my thing, and went home. A week later that same friend, Gary, called and asked if I remembered meeting a girl named Sandra Walker while I was on the Tech campus. Being that I was single and there were only a half dozen or so coeds at the Bible study that night, I assumed I had probably met her (or tried to), but I wasn't sure which one she was. Well, that didn't matter to Gary; he was sure I should "remeet" her, and he gave me her number. To be honest, I wasn't in a hurry to call because I wasn't really sure whom I was calling. But eventually I made the call. She agreed to go out. So we set a date and time, and I went on about my business.

Let me pause the story here. I'm sure you already know where this is going. And I'm equally sure you have a similar story of your own. Or you want to anyway. But this pregnant pause illustrates the point of this chapter. More important, it illustrates this crazy dynamic that is constantly intersecting with our experience.

I was happily single. Very happily single. Moving back to Atlanta had turned out to be a good move for me. I liked my job. I had an income-producing hobby. And I liked my single problems much better than the married problems I kept hearing about. But at this point I was days away from having every facet of my life re-directed—I just didn't know it. That first date with Sandra was going to impact my financial path, my professional path, my relational path. Everything was about to change. Why? Because about two hours after she walked out of her dorm and got into my car, she captured—as in captured to the tenth power—my attention. I didn't *give* her my attention. I wasn't trying to *pay* attention. She *took* it from me and never gave it back. And once she had my attention, she won my affection, which drastically altered my direction. And that was a good thing. But I wasn't expecting it.

I'm sure you can relate. We've all had those kinds of defining moments when we're just going along, doing our own thing, and then—*whoa . . . what's that over there?* When it happens, it is an extremely powerful thing. Veering out of my lane in the direction of Sandra is a positive example of this principle. But let's face it: like every principle, this one can work for us or against us.

All of us have people or events or opportunities in our past that reflect the much-more-frequent flip side. Looking back, there are people you wish you had never met. Relationships you wish you'd never initiated. Numbers you wish you'd never called. Voice mails you wish you'd never acknowledged. Business "opportunities" you wish you had ignored. Life was better before these things grabbed your attention. In many cases, the path you were on before they came along was the path you should have adhered to. But you didn't. And what grabbed your attention altered your direction.

No doubt you had a mental conversation that went something like this:

Wow . . . would you look at that.
I probably shouldn't go there . . .
But perhaps I should double-check to make sure I shouldn't go there . . .
Yeah, I shouldn't go there.
C'mon now, focus.
Probably wouldn't hurt to go there for a moment.

Remember how common sense seemed to get railroaded by the emotion of whatever or whoever it was that grabbed your attention?

139

Before you knew it, you were moving in an entirely different direction. Usually there is a strong emotional appeal to the things that capture our attention. We get sucked in to those detours because something emotionally engaging is on those paths. My observation is that the things that tend to grab or capture my attention are often things I should avoid. Advertisers make a living trying to capture my attention. And that's okay. Everybody needs to eat and live indoors. Great advertisements appeal to our emotions. Let's face it: malls and car dealerships are not emotionally neutral environments. But often the things that grab our attention lead to regret.

What captures our attention influences our direction. Attention, direction, destination. That's the principle of the path in three words. And as your attention goes, so goes your life.

THE APPEAL OF ATTENTION

Unlike my black Lab, whose attention seems to be genetically locked in on food, we have a choice. I don't think Shadow really has a choice. Seems as if she can't help but follow her nose and her appetite. She is distracted by everything with a food-related scent. This has sent her in some not-so-pleasant directions. As you might be aware, people like to give their pastors food. Actually, food and ties. Since I rarely wear a tie, we get lots of food. Especially at Christmas. People are generous and gracious. That means they bring large quantities, and they don't bother us by ringing the doorbell or even knocking. They just leave things by the front door. Or so they say. We don't know for sure because we don't get to see what they brought. We just see traces of what they brought. We know someone has brought us a perishable gift because there are usually bits of paper and ribbon scattered around the front lawn. When we are able to locate a card, we write a thank-you note. But we are always vague because we aren't ever sure what we are saying thank you for. Maybe we should ask Shadow to write the notes. If you are a dog person, you've probably heard that chocolate and caffeine will kill your dog. Not true. It will keep her up late into the night. But it won't kill 'er. At least that has been our experience.

But we, unlike our friends in the animal kingdom, can choose to *give* our attention to things. You and I are not necessarily ruled by the things that grab or capture our attention. We certainly can be and have been. But we have a choice. We can *give* our attention to anything we choose to give it to. And that means we have the potential to harness this amazing principle to our benefit. If attention determines direction, and we can choose what or who gets our attention, then that gives us a lot of leverage concerning our future.

Whereas *emotion* fuels the things that grab our attention, *intentionality* fuels our decision to give certain things our attention. And I bet you would agree, the things that we choose to give our attention to are generally better for us and set us up for success in the future. Once again: attention, direction, destination.

A Really Big Deal

Looking back, I imagine there are things you wish you had given more attention to: Your health. Your grades. The way you handled your money. Your marriage. What was going on in the lives of your kids. Maybe you wish you had given more attention to your spiritual life at certain points. Your life would be better, richer, and more enjoyable if less of your attention had been hijacked from the things you should have been focusing on.

Your life would be different if your *parents* had chosen to give more attention to certain things. The reach of this principle extends beyond your life or lifetime. The things you give your attention to will influence the direction and destination of everyone in your circle of influence. Looking back on your own experience, that's probably undeniable. So then, why are we so easily distracted? Why don't we consistently *give* our attention to the things that merit our attention?

Interestingly enough, there is a phrase we heard just about every day growing up that answers that question: *pay attention!*

Pay attention, class!

Pay attention, son!

Are you paying attention?

If you had been paying attention, you wouldn't have made such a mess.

Chances are, nobody has demanded that you *pay attention* lately. They may have thought it. Actually, I have that thought every Sunday morning. But the use of that imperative is generally limited to home and school. It is, however, a loaded phrase. Why would we associate the term *pay* with the term *attention*? Why does a teacher have to tell a student who is staring out the window at a bird on the windowsill to *pay attention*? Why *pay*? Pay implies *price*. Pay implies *cost*. Pay implies giving away something of value. Loss. And it is this sense of loss that keeps us from paying attention to the things that deserve our attention and would serve us best in the future.

The reason you don't pay better attention to your health is because doing so will cost you something. You would be forced to give up something you enjoy. The reason your neighbor isn't paying more attention to his kids is because it feels like a payment. He would be forced to give up something else. Something that has captured his attention. It is the cost associated with paying attention to the right things that makes it so difficult to do.

When we pay for something, we expect to receive something of equal or greater value in return. And that is precisely what happens when we pay attention to the right things. You probably have plenty of experiences to validate that idea. If you graduated from high school, you've seen this dynamic at work. You received a diploma because you paid attention to school rather than allowing other things to capture your attention. And if your high school experience was anything like mine, I bet there were plenty of distractions. Fortunately for most of us, there were people in our lives during that season who kept reminding us to *pay attention* to what mattered most. Once high school is in the rearview mirror, the voices of reason disappear pretty quickly. The battle for our attention becomes severe. But it is an important battle to monitor, because it is a battle for the future. Again, as our attention goes, so go our lives.

The *capture*-versus-*pay* dynamic explains a great deal of what we observe in our culture and in our lives. It is a tension we are forced to deal with every day on several fronts. We encounter it relationally, financially, professionally, and spiritually. In every arena of life, there are things vying for our attention. There are people and activities that have the potential to lure us away from the things to which we should be *paying* attention. And if we are honest, the cost of disentangling ourselves from unhealthy relationships and activities seems too high a price to pay. And at the same time, the benefits associated with *paying* attention to the right things seem so distant that they don't whet our appetite for change. And so we continue to live our lives captive to the things that have captured our attention.

This tension is so central to the human experience that it should come as no surprise that we find it addressed in the Scriptures. What may astound you is the frequency with which it is referenced. Just about every one of the more than three dozen authors of the Old and New Testaments alludes to or speaks directly about this principle. Over and over, God reminds us that the things to which we harness our attention direct our lives; whatever captures our attention will determine our destination.

For the sake of time, space, and interest, I'll only cite five examples. The first passage is found in the book of Deuteronomy. Here's a bit of context. The people of Israel were about to go into the Holy Land and take it as their own. But before they moved in and set up their new society, God gave the nation a system of laws to live by. And when he had finished outlining how they were to conduct themselves in their new home, he said:

> If you pay attention to these laws and are careful to follow them,
> then the LORD your God will keep his covenant of love with you,
> as he swore to your forefathers. (7:12)

There it is: "pay attention." God knew that once Israel settled their new land, they would become enamored with the customs and conduct of the surrounding nations. He knew that there were elements in those pagan cultures that had the potential to capture his people's attention. So God instructed them to "pay attention" to the customs and conduct he set out. Notice as well the subtle reference to the path principle. He said "If you . . . are careful to follow them . . ." God laid out a direction with a specific destination. In this case, national adherence to the law would result in divine blessing. And later he would clarify the consequence of abandoning his law as well. The path of disobedience would lead to divine disciplinary action. Specifically, invasion from the very nations they chose to emulate. Either way, the direction they chose would determine their destination. And what the nation chose to give their attention to would ultimately determine which path they chose.

Years later—many, many years later—the second king of Israel, David, referenced this principle as well. Listen to his request of God in Psalm 119: 35: "Direct me in the path of your commands, for there I find delight."

Then in verse 37 he adds: "Turn my eyes"—which throughout Scripture is a metaphor for one's attention—"away from worthless things."

Think about that statement: "God, please turn my eyes away from worthless things." Why? Because if I focus on worthless things, I'll be drawn in the direction of worthless things.

Every one of us can think of a time when our attention got fixed on something that turned out to be a waste of time. In David's words, a "worthless" thing. David knew about that all too well. So he asked, "Please, God, I want my eyes to be fixed on things that matter."

Then look at the last part of verse 37: "Preserve my life according to your word." In other words, "I don't want to end up at some stage of life and think, *How in the world did I get here?* Preserve my life by helping me to turn my gaze, my eyes, my attention away from worthless things."

That is a powerful verse. One worth committing to memory. For not a day goes by that we are not tempted to allow our minds, our eyes, our attention to drift toward and run the risk of being captured by worthless things. Things that have the potential to lure us down paths we will regret taking.

David's son Solomon weighed in on this too. In Proverbs 4:25 he wrote, "Let your eyes look straight ahead, fix your gaze directly before you." In other words, don't allow yourself to be distracted by things that have the potential to capture your attention, things that have the power to draw your focus away from those things to which your attention would be fastened. Decide ahead of time to pay attention to those things that need and deserve your attention. This is a great verse to memorize if you have a difficult time disciplining your eyes. Several of my friends who travel for a living quote this verse as they walk through the airport terminal. And I have other friends who have suggested their wives quote this verse when they are at the mall . . . but for entirely different reasons. For reasons I can't explain, unhealthy distractions are generally to our left and to our right, rather than straight ahead. So this is good advice regardless of where we are.

Hundreds of years after the reign of King Solomon, Jesus showed up and gave us his version of the principle of the path:

The eye is the lamp of the body. If your eyes are good, your whole body will be full of light. But if your eyes are bad, your whole body will be full of darkness." (Matt. 6:22–23)

In Bible times, since people didn't have electricity, they carried oil lamps when they walked at night. If you've ever been camping and used a Coleman lantern, you know the drill: you walk with the lantern either in front of you or maybe holding it on a stick, because the farther the light is in front of you, the farther you can see. There is a sense in which the light leads the way.

Jesus is saying, "Your eye—what you see, gaze at, and pay attention to—is like the lantern of your entire life. It lights or leads your way. As your body follows a light in the dark, so your life follows what your eye focuses on." With that in mind, take another look at the second part of the verse: "If your eyes are good,"—the Greek word translated *good* actually means "wholesome, pure, or healthy"—"your whole body will be full of light." As you may know, the term *light* in the New Testament is used to denote something good or divine. Jesus' point? If your eyes are focused on good things, your body will be led in a good direction. But as you might expect, there is a second half of this equation as well. "But if your eyes are bad, your whole body will be full of darkness. If then the light within you is darkness, how great is that darkness!" (Matt. 6:23). As your eyes (or focus) go, so goes your life. As your attention goes, so goes your life. For good or for bad. The things you give your attention to function as the directional beacon for your life. Attention establishes direction, which determines destination.

I could fill another dozen or so pages with biblical references to support this simple equation, but I doubt you need more convincing. If you are like me, the problem is not a lack of understanding as much as it is a lack of application.

TRUE FOR YOU

Now, as I have said over and over in this book, it is so easy to see these principles at work in the lives of other people. In fact, you may be thinking, *Oh, I wish my cousin or daughter or ex would read this.* And perhaps she should. But if she gets that opportunity, would you come to her mind as she came to yours? For the time being, let's not worry about all the people who might need to read this and instead focus on the one who actually has. That would be you.

If it is true that we will steer our lives toward the people and things that have captured our attention, then perhaps we should spend our next few minutes together exploring the list of people and things that have captured *your* attention. Even if you don't plan on making any changes, you owe it to yourself to know what and who it is that's directing your life. Up until this point, you haven't really thought about these . . . these distractions . . . as being anything other than distractions. But they are, in fact, directing your life. To use Jesus' imagery, they are functioning as the light on your path. So you should at least know what or who they are. After all, there is a sense in which you have turned your future over to them. And you have, in a sense, turned the future of anyone you are responsible for over to them as well.

So what about you? You are aware of how easy it is to become distracted by things that have no business being a part of your life. You know that from your own past experience. But what about now? What has your attention now? Who has your attention now? Has anything or anyone captured your attention that has no business being a part of your life now? Be honest. There's no one to lie to at this precise moment but yourself. Right now it's just *you* and *you*. You may feel like I'm part of the discussion, but I'm not. I'm really not a part of the conversation at all. So there is nothing to be gained by being defensive. There is no point repeating your well-rehearsed excuses to the pages of this book. Just be honest. As we discussed earlier, self-deception doesn't accomplish anything. It, too, is a path. And it doesn't lead to a hammock by the sea.

Has anything or anyone captured your attention or affection in a way that is distracting you from the things or people that deserve your attention? Are you giving an inordinate amount of attention to something that a year ago wasn't even on your radar screen? Is there anyone you are giving attention to that, if it were to become public information, would be a bit embarrassing . . . or worse? Do your spouse or kids feel like they are competing for time that should be given to them anyway? Is there a distraction that began as a small thing that has become less small with time? Is there a distraction that took a little of your time at first but now consumes an inordinate amount of time? Is there a hobby or pastime that began as a small expense but is now a significant line item in your personal finances? Is there anything dividing your mind at work? Home? Church? Am I starting to get on your nerves?

Okay, let's ask the same questions a different way. Is there something or someone you need to begin paying more attention to? Is there something clamoring for your attention that deserves your attention—and instead of doing the right thing, you are making excuses? What are you putting off? What is it you just don't find the time to get around to because of the other, less important stuff? Your education? Kids? Spiritual pursuits? Saving more? Getting out of debt? Your health? Your parents? Think. Be honest. Much is at stake! We don't drift in good directions. We discipline and prioritize ourselves there.

What about your marriage? Is that something that you need to give more attention to? Culture argues that once you say "I do," it's time to hit autopilot—as if good marriages fly by themselves. But they don't. Bet you already knew that.

What about the spiritual development of your kids? If you've got kids, this is something you've got to pay attention to. Seemingly few parents do. And the earlier the better. I know too many parents who treat their kids like their automobiles. They wait for the red light on the dashboard to light up before giving them any attention. Preventive maintenance will help you avoid emergencies with your kids and your cars. But in both instances, it is something you have to pay attention to. (Not to turn this into a chapter on parenting, but if you're waiting until your kids are fourteen or fifteen to get them in an environment that will engage them in the development of their faith, you are going to be sorely disappointed in the results. Spiritual development operates like the principle of the harvest. You sow early and reap later. You can't cram for a harvest like you cram for a test. Adolescence is when parents begin to reap what they have sown. It is not the time to begin sowing. Unfortunately, too many parents don't pay attention to this aspect of their children's lives until they have missed the opportunity to do it right. A good student ministry will not make up for years of spiritual neglect. Parental guidance is definitely required.)

The point is, you don't have to be yanked around by your emotions and passions. You choose what you give your attention to. So, what do you need to give more attention to now?

FRIENDS TO AVOID

If nothing is coming to mind, how 'bout we run that same question through yet another filter. In the past six months, has anyone approached you or, more to the point, confronted you about a relationship or lifestyle issue? Does your spouse keep bringing up the same stuff over and over? Have you heard something along the lines of, "I really think you are spending too much time with . . ." "I have noticed that you . . ." "Didn't you just . . ." "Haven't you already . . . ?"

Have you heard yourself getting defensive over stuff that you swear is "really no big deal"? If it's no big deal, where's all that emotion coming from? Could it be there are people who are more concerned about the direction of your life than you are? Are you responding to their concerns about where you are heading with statements that simply describe where you are now? What's going on *now*?

Remember how your parents would overreact to something you did or were doing? Now that you are a bit older, perhaps you can understand why parents do that. If you *are* a parent, I know you understand. Parents don't respond to where their children are—they respond to where they see their kids headed. Why? Because parents know that what grabs the wheel of their children's attention will eventually steer the course of their children's lives. So they—we—overreact. I think God made us that way. So who in your life seems to be overreacting? Who's focused on where you are headed, opposed to where you are? What do they see that you can't, or won't? Why won't you pay attention?

NOT A DAY TO WASTE

Like everything we've talked about so far, the relationship between attention and direction *will* impact your life, regardless of whether or not you accept or act on it. Principles are dynamic and dumb in that way. They don't get offended. They don't quit. They don't really care what we think. They just keep on going, working behind the scenes to shape our lives.

That being the case, whatever or whoever it is that has captured your attention is at this very moment influencing the direction of your life—for good or not so good. And whatever or whoever it is that you have *chosen* to give your attention to is influencing the direction of your life as well. But now that you are aware of how all this works, you have the opportunity to embrace this principle and leverage it for your benefit. Now you are in a position to choose your destination rather than discovering it once you arrive. But choosing will require change. And change does not come easy, especially when it requires us to redirect our attention away from people and things that have a strong emotional grip on us.

The author of the book of Hebrews summed it up this way, "We must pay more careful attention, therefore, to what we have heard, so that we do not drift away" (2:1). This New Testament author was addressing a Jewish audience whose attention had been diverted away from the teachings of Christ. They had begun to *drift*. They were careening toward things that had captured their attention. Like a good driver's ed teacher, the author urged his readers to get their eyes back on the road in front of them, lest they leave the road entirely. That was his way of saying what we've said throughout this chapter. Attention determines direction, and direction determines destination.

There is a reason the Scriptures reiterate this principle over and over. God cares about the direction of your life. Think about that for a moment. God . . . as in GOD . . . is concerned about the direction and quality of your life. And though we've never met, I'm guessing *you* are concerned about the direction and quality of your life as well. So that's one important thing you and God have in common. It might be the only thing you have in common, but at least there's that. And *that* is no unimportant thing. So here's something to consider. If you and God care about your future, why resist him? If it has become clear to you that there are things or people you need to pay less attention to and things or people that deserve more of your attention, why not give in to that? Why resist what you know is true and right for you? Why not, in this very moment, enlist God's help in bringing about the change both you and your heavenly Father desire?

If your response to all of this is something along the lines of, "Wait a minute; who said anything about resisting God? I may be guilty of a bit of misprioritizing, but I don't have anything against God," here's something to consider. When we resist God's will for our lives, we are in essence resisting God. When we resist the priorities he has established for us through Scripture, we resist him. When we resist taking full responsibility for the people he has entrusted to our care, we resist him. When we are poor stewards with the financial resources he has entrusted to us, we resist him. Subtle, I know. But it is still there. Every time I feel resistance from one of my kids over how to approach homework, I'm reminded of similar tugs-of-will I have with God.

By now you know the shifts in affection and attention you need to make. And you know this will be no easy task. If these were easy changes to make, you would have already made them. So perhaps now is the time to lay down any resistance you've had to God's will in your life and invite his help. And if you do, you will discover that in shifting your attention to the things that please your heavenly Father, you will actually be shifting your attention *toward* your heavenly Father. Something wonderful happens when the resistance is gone. Something relational happens when the resistance is gone. And in the end, that is what your heavenly Father desires above all else.

If you don't remember anything else from this chapter, I hope you will remember this: as your attention goes, so goes your life. So pay careful attention to what you are paying attention to. Pay attention to the things that are competing for your attention. Pause before devoting your attention to anything. And devote special attention to those things that deserve your attention. For as Jesus said, your eye is the lamp of your entire body. And if your eyes are good, your whole body will be full of light.

TEN

ROAD CLOSED

The subtitle of this book implies that there is always a way to get from where you are to where you want to be. But we both know that that's not always the case. We can retrace our steps, but we can't turn back the hands of the clock. We can make better choices "next time," but we can't go back and do anything about the first time. Time, bad decisions, and experience put some destinations out of reach. There are dreams that can't come true. There are fortunes that are lost for good. There are relationships that can't be fully mended. There are scars we can't hide. There are chapters that can't be torn out and rewritten. So as we conclude our journey together, I want to answer the question, *What do you do with the dreams that can't come true?* Or to put it in terms more consistent with our theme, *What do you do when it dawns on you that there are destinations you will never reach?* What do you do when factors outside your control make it impossible to get from where you are to where you want to be?

As the pastor of a large congregation, not a week of my life goes by that I am not invited into someone's personal pain and disappointment. I've buried babies, teenagers, moms, dads, brothers, and sisters—many of whom were friends as well as parishioners. I've walked with men and women through bitter divorces and child custody battles. I've counseled couples through bankruptcy. I've sat with parents as they grappled with the news that their son or daughter was gay. And I've sat up late at night with gay friends as they contemplated their futures and the rejection of their families. I've talked to pregnant teenagers who were terrified to tell their parents. On several occasions I've been the one to deliver news that I knew would rock the recipient's world to the core. And each time, that person's path changed irreversibly.

Some destinations are unreachable. Some dreams won't come true. Some dreams can't come true. Some destinations become unreachable because of lifestyle choices. Some are unreachable because of a single decision. Some destinations are out of reach because of mistakes we've made. Some are out of reach because of decisions others made. Sometimes we are to blame. Sometimes there is no one to blame. In time, the reason behind our inability to get where we want to be becomes irrelevant. We are where we *are*, we aren't where we want to be—and there is nothing that can be done to change that.

I believe everybody faces this kind of disappointment at some point. Time is often the culprit. Vince Lombardi, the famed coach of the Green Bay Packers, was quoted as saying, "We didn't lose;

we just ran out of time." Perhaps with unlimited time we could make more of our dreams come true. If we could stop the clock, we might be able to reach any destination we choose. But there aren't any time-outs in life. The clock is always running. At some point we wake to the realization that *it*—whatever *it* is—is not going to happen for us.

As if that weren't bad enough, you look around and it appears that *it* is happening for everybody around you. Everybody else seems to be living your dream. Everybody else seems to be arriving at your destination. Everybody but you. Everybody else seems to be on schedule with the American dream. Everybody else's family seems to get along. You hear coworkers talking about their great vacations and you think, *I can't take a great vacation because I'm still paying on the two previous ones.* Everybody else's car is always a bit cleaner and newer. You've been in five weddings—but none of them were yours. You ask yourself, *When do I get to be in my own wedding?* You've got a closet full of useless dresses or a drawer full of useless groomsmen's gifts that memorialize your singleness.

Or perhaps you are at the other end of that spectrum. Your first marriage is unraveling. The handwriting isn't on the divorce papers yet, but it is certainly on the wall. The dream of finishing life with your partner is not going to come true. You are about to be single again. Or a single parent. And maybe the whole thing is your spouse's fault. Or maybe it's yours, but at this point it doesn't matter. You aren't where you hoped to be.

Perhaps your unfulfillable dream revolves around children. Specifically, your inability to have them. In your mind, the future was all about kids. But as it stands, there aren't going to be any family vacations. At least not the way you imagined them. There aren't going to be any recitals, ball games, or good-night kisses. And it is tearing your heart out.

Maybe your frustration revolves around your career track. Or maybe that's the problem. There hasn't really been a track. There have just been *jobs*. Job after job. Somehow you've never been able to get the traction other people have. And you feel left behind. You stopped going to class reunions years ago because you got tired of exaggerating.

I may have skipped your area of conflict. But you've got one. Everybody has disappointments. Everybody knows of a destination they can't reach, a dream that can't come true. And these are extraordinarily emotional issues for most of us. So emotional that you have a difficult time even going there in your mind. Perhaps you are even tempted to skip this last section and move on to whatever's next on your reading list. That's understandable. But I hope you won't. Because sometimes it is the destinations that are out of our reach that create the circumstances God uses to remind us that we are never out of *his* reach.

Speaking of God, perhaps it's the God part of the equation that makes your disappointment so . . . disappointing. You feel like God made you a promise and didn't come through. You're convinced that the destination you set your sights on was a destination God placed in your heart. You're convinced that the dream that can't come true is not just your dream. It was God's dream for you. And now, at a time when you desperately need to lean hard on your heavenly Father, you aren't sure he can be trusted.

Perhaps you aren't sure he's there at all. And you are hoping I don't suggest you pray—because you've already done *that*. In fact, you've done everything you know to do, and in spite of your best efforts, certain destinations remain out of reach.

FROM HERE TO THERE

The realization that some destinations are out of reach often elicits very powerful emotions. Dangerous emotions. The kinds of emotions that drive people toward behaviors that put their dreams even farther out of reach. Worse, I've seen the emotions fueled by disappointment drive individuals into behaviors that put others' destinations out of reach as well. I've seen the emotions associated with the loss of a child drive men and women into a cycle of substance abuse that eventually destroyed their marriages. I've seen job loss drive men so deep into depression that they alienated their kids. The fear of remaining single can drive women into relationships that leave them with secrets and scars that lead them even further away from where they've always wanted to be. If someone intentionally stole your dream, professionally or relationally, I imagine you've given some thought to how you could steal his or hers as well. Our prison system is full of men and women whose quest for revenge ensured that none of their dreams would come true. Their current destination is the last place on earth they would have chosen. But there they are. Why? Because disappointment creates powerful emotions.

I imagine you have stories you could tell. No family or individual is immune to the waves of emotion that follow the realization that a dream won't come true, that a destination is out of reach. So what are we supposed to do?

NOT THE FIRST

One of the things I love about Scripture is that the narratives we find there incorporate the entire spectrum of human experience and emotion. Scripture stands as a reminder that regardless of what we've experienced, we are not the first. Regardless of what we feel, someone else has navigated through that fog before us. And more important, someone has faced what we've faced, felt what we've felt, and his or her faith has survived. Think about your favorite Bible character. My hunch is that this individual is your favorite because of his response to circumstances he would have never chosen, circumstances that in some way put a legitimate destination out of reach. No doubt your favorite Bible story revolves around conflict, disappointment, and, most important, God's faithfulness. So let me walk you through an incident from the life of David that serves as an example of how to respond to the inevitable disappointments in life. I chose this particular story because it is extreme. But in spite of the gamut of emotions David was left to sort through, he did not despair. If God can be found and trusted in these circumstances, certainly he can be trusted in yours and mine.

This series of events took place while David was king of Israel. He was probably close to fifty at the time and had been Israel's king for quite a while. He had many children by several wives. He had conquered all of his enemies. He had a legacy, a future, and a promise from God. But unbeknownst to him, he was weeks away from an event that would set off a string of events involving his children that would put something very important to him out of reach. So let's begin.

David's firstborn son was named Amnon. By all rights, he would be heir to the throne of Israel. Unfortunately, he fell in love with his half sister, Tamar. As is the case today, that kind of relationship was not looked upon favorably, and besides being outside of what was socially acceptable, it was illegal. But Amnon was lovesick. Literally. The scripture tells us, "Amnon became so obsessed with Tamar that he became ill" (2 Sam. 13:2 NLT). So he devised a plan that would allow him to be alone with Tamar in order to see how far he could take the relationship. He pretended to be sick, and through his father, David, he invited Tamar to prepare a meal for him. When she had finished, Amnon sent all the servants out of the house and asked his sister to come into his bedroom to feed him. When she did, he grabbed her and begged her to come to bed with him. She refused, saying that such a thing would be a disgrace to her and Amnon. However, Amnon refused to be dissuaded and raped Tamar. Then he called for his servants and had her thrown out of his house in disgrace.

When word of this reached David, he was furious. But he did nothing. Nothing! Why? We will never know. Perhaps it was because Amnon was his heir, and to punish him according to the law would have made this evil act public knowledge. Perhaps he felt his affair with Bathsheba removed his right to confront his son for a similar breach of integrity. Whatever the case, he did nothing to defend his daughter's honor or punish his son. He just let it go.

And that unwise decision set the stage for the next unfortunate series of events.

Tamar went to her brother Absalom for help and protection. When Absalom heard her story, he, too, was furious. But unlike his father, he decided to do something about it. Of all David's children, Absalom was the most like his father. He was a natural-born leader; he was handsome, charismatic, and patient. He waited two years before acting in his sister's defense. But when he did, he did it up in the grandest fashion. He threw a party for all his brothers and sisters, including Amnon. Once they had gathered, eaten, and drunk enough wine to dull their senses, Absalom signaled for his men to enter the banquet hall and murder Amnon in front of everyone present. The remaining family members fled the house, assuming Absalom's intent was to kill all of them. But his feud was with Amnon alone. And once he had avenged the rape, he fled across the border to a little town called Geshar, in the vicinity of modern-day Syria.

When news of the murder reached David, he wept. And understandably so. His entire world was different now. In a single night he'd lost two sons. He lost his heir to the throne. And he lost the son with whom he had the most in common, the son who—of all his children—was most suited to be king. To complicate things further, David knew it was his responsibility to avenge the death of his firstborn by arresting Absalom and punishing him according to the law. But once again, David did nothing. He just let it go.

Three years went by, and the Bible tells us that David and Absalom began to miss each other. So Joab, the captain of David's army, worked it out for Absalom to reenter the country and move back to Jerusalem—the capital city—to be near his father. But once Absalom was back in the city, David never called for him. Absalom was confused, to say the least, so he called for Joab in order to get some kind of explanation, but Joab didn't respond to his request. After a couple of unanswered messages, Absalom had Joab's field set on fire. When Joab discovered who was behind the vandalism, he went to confront Absalom. But Absalom demanded an audience with his father, and at last a meeting of father and son was arranged. With all the detail we are given about the events leading up to the meeting, one would think that the author would include a detailed account of what took place when these two powerful personalities were reunited. Instead, the entire event is summarized in two sentences.

Then the king summoned Absalom, and he came in and bowed down with his face to the ground before the king. And the king kissed Absalom. (2 Sam. 14:33)

That's it. Formal. Short. Not at all what Absalom was looking for. Not at all what Absalom was hoping for. And from what the scripture tells us, that was the last time they saw each other. We can only speculate as to why David was not able or willing to bridge the gap between himself and his son. The father-son relationship can be difficult in the healthiest of families. But with all the baggage these two men were carrying, it is somewhat understandable why things didn't go well that day. And based on what happened next, it is even more clear that things really didn't go well that day at all.

Absalom never recovered from his father's unwillingness to reconcile their relationship. His bitterness soon expressed itself as a desire for revenge. But Absalom was not one to react impulsively; he was ever the patient man. So for the next four years he simply sat by the main gate of Jerusalem and made himself available to the common folk. He acted as judge and advisor. His judiciousness, accessibility, and charisma were the talk of the city and, eventually, the kingdom. In time, he won the hearts of the populace. They began to see in Absalom the leader they once had in his father, the aging and now distant king.

At the end of four years, Absalom made his move. He went to Hebron, a city thirty kilometers from Jerusalem, and had himself proclaimed king. As it turns out, this announcement was only one part of an elaborate plan to overthrow his father and replace him as king. Absalom's followers, in concert, rose up all over the nation to proclaim that Israel had a new king. The author of 2 Samuel summarized it this way: "And so the conspiracy gained strength, and Absalom's following kept on increasing" (2 Sam. 15:12).

IRRETRIEVABLE

There will be moments in all our lives when we receive news that, in an instant, alters our future irreversibly. Information that serves as a stake through the heart of our dreams. I've delivered that news more times than I can remember. And I've received my share.

In the moments that follow, we are lost. We are lost because a part of what defined the future for us is gone. It is hard to imagine the future without someone you've loved for twenty or thirty years. It is difficult to find your bearings when a career track vanishes with the arrival of an e-mail. It is one thing to talk about divorce; it is something quite different to be served papers. Perhaps your future went dark the day you discovered you were pregnant—or that your daughter was.

The news of Absalom's rebellion was all of that and more for David. If there had been any hope for reconciliation, any hope that his son would succeed him as king, it was gone. That was a destination now completely out of reach. It would never happen.

When messengers brought David news of the rebellion, he responded as a defeated man. He announced that he was abandoning the city. He was walking away from the capital city and his throne. His explanation was that he feared that staying would turn Jerusalem into a battlefield and that the civilian population would suffer unnecessarily. And no doubt that was true. But as the story unfolds, we discover that David did not want to fight his son. There was nothing to be gained for him in that. What he wanted was completely out of reach. So he and his entire household, along with that portion of the army still loyal to him, packed hurriedly and fled the capital. As they exited the city, the author tells us that "the whole countryside wept aloud" (2 Sam. 15:23).

Just outside the walls of the city an exchange took place between David and a high priest that gives us a window into the king's soul at this defining moment in his life. When Zadok, the high priest at that time, heard David was leaving the city, he organized a group of priests to accompany David and to take with them the ark of the covenant. This was a significant gesture, as the ark represented the presence and blessing of God. The assumption was that whichever side in this conflict (or any conflict) possessed the ark was assured victory. It must have been extraordinarily frightening for the citizens of Jerusalem to see the ark leaving the city. In their lifetimes, no one had defeated an army that carried the ark of God. In their superstitious way of thinking, it was as though God were abandoning them as well. It was a sign that God was with David and that Absalom and all who stood with him would face certain defeat. For David, Zadok's decision should have come as great encouragement. Seeing the ark on the move could be interpreted in only one way. David was blameless in God's sight, and thus he would be vindicated in the end.

But David didn't see it that way; perhaps that was why he never gave the command to move the ark to begin with. He was prepared to leave it behind. Not because he lacked faith in God, or because he did not see himself as one who needed God's presence. There was something else going on inside David. So, in a move that no one would have anticipated, he commanded Zadok to take the ark back into the city. And though the king owed the priest no explanation for his decision, he explained himself anyway.

As you read his reason for leaving the ark behind, keep in mind that this was a man who was walking away from everything. Everything that mattered had been taken from him. His future was dark. The only thing he knew for certain was there were dreams that could no longer come true: His firstborn son was dead. His daughter's honor was gone forever. His relationship with Absalom was lost. The unity of the kingdom had been destroyed. His reputation had been irreparably damaged. And he was about to go to war against a portion of his own army, led by his own son. The only things he was certain of were bad.

So why not take the ark?

> Then the king said to Zadok, "Take the ark of God back into the city. If I find favor in the LORD's eyes, he will bring me back and let me see it and his dwelling place again. But if he says, 'I am not pleased with you,' then I am ready; let him do to me whatever seems good to him." (2 Sam. 15:25–26)

If David had learned anything in his years as shepherd, fugitive, and king, it was this: God can be trusted but not manipulated. The lights may have gone out on David's future and his dreams, but not on his faith. Removing the ark from Jerusalem would be nothing more than an act of desperation, an effort to force God's hand. David knew better. He had learned better. He would not try to bargain with God. In spite of his desperate circumstances, he would not abandon his faith in God. And he would not try to manipulate the loyalty of the citizenry by carting off the ark. Instead, David decided to accept whatever the future held as if it came directly from the hand of God: "Let him do to me whatever seems good to him."

David wasn't being fatalistic or passive. There were still decisions to be made and a war to be fought. But he was willing to accept the outcome, whatever it was, as the will of God. There were perhaps even more dreams that he would be forced to abandon. But he would not abandon his faith.

THE JERUSALEM MOMENT

I believe everybody has a Jerusalem experience at some point in his or her journey. There comes a time in each of our lives when we are forced to turn our backs on something we hoped for, prayed for, dreamed about, and perhaps planned for. These are usually good things. But a day comes when we are faced with the reality that they're not going to happen for us. We aren't going to get there. That dream isn't coming true.

These are defining moments. For some, they signal the end of faith. The disappointment crushes all hope that God can be counted on in the future. Some panic and do things that only make a bad situation worse. Others bargain with God, looking for a way to force his hand. But for many this is where faith begins. Their Jerusalem moment forces them to face the reality that they have no control over the future and that their only hope is in the Lord.

Even as I type these words, my mind is flooded with memories of conversations I've had and letters I've received from men, women, and teenagers whose broken dreams and broken hearts led them to the place where they could say with David, "Let him do to me whatever seems good to him." These are individuals who have learned one of the most difficult lessons of life. Namely, when it dawns on you that your dreams can't come true, the best response is to lean hard into your heavenly Father—even when it appears that he is responsible for your disappointment. The only other option is to run from the only one who can bring comfort when you need comfort the most. So David sent Zadok back into the city with the ark. He chose to trust the very God who could have kept all his troubles from happening in the first place. He chose to lean hard into the one from whose hand he accepted all that had and was about to transpire. As David led his loyal subjects up the Mount of Olives and away from the city, he wept. His head was covered, and he was barefoot. These were signs of mourning. He was a defeated man. He had lost everything he considered dear. Everything except his faith.

Sometime later, perhaps that same day, Absalom entered Jerusalem and claimed his father's throne. No doubt Absalom expected his father to stay and defend the city. Now he was left with the unenviable task of chasing his father and his father's army through the open countryside. All the military leaders who advised Absalom knew this would put David at a distinct advantage, because as a young general David had spent years fighting in the open. But Absalom had no choice. To solidify his kingship, his father and his father's army had to be defeated.

So Absalom and the army of Israel went in pursuit of David. David's army ambushed Absalom and his army in the forest of Ephraim. It was a rout. More than twenty thousand men died in that single day of combat. David had ordered his generals to capture Absalom alive. But when David's senior general discovered the young man, he ignored David's command and killed Absalom. The scripture does not tell us why Joab disobeyed David's command; it was a dangerous thing to do. And there were witnesses present. Perhaps it was because Joab had had a front-row seat to David's unwillingness to discipline his children. Perhaps he feared that once again David would do nothing. So he took that responsibility into his own hands. Twenty thousand Israelites had died that day. Perhaps Joab couldn't bear the thought of Absalom going unpunished. So he did what he knew David could not.

When David received news of his son's death, he was crushed. Here is where we discover the depth of David's love for Absalom. As he wept, he was overheard saying, "O my son Absalom! My son, my son Absalom! If only I had died instead of you—O Absalom, my son, my son!" (2 Sam. 18:33). Absalom was a traitor, a murderer, and an insurrectionist. He was responsible for the deaths of thousands of Israelites. But in spite of all that, David would have traded his own life for his son's. When he lost Absalom, he lost a part of himself that he would never be able to recover. This was not the way it was supposed to be. This was not the future as he had foreseen it. Yet this was what happened. And he chose to receive it as coming from the hand of his heavenly Father: "Let him do to me whatever seems good to him."

CHOICES

Sandra and I had a friend named Debbie Kennedy who died of cancer several years ago. She was a remarkable woman. She never married, though she sure desired that. She never had kids, though she was an incredible second mom to a number of children. She served in ministry her entire adult life. She had a joy that went beyond contagious—it was infectious. You couldn't be around Debbie without smiling. She underwent several surgeries, chemo, radiation, the whole nine yards. She was supported by friends, but no family. Toward the end she said something to me that I'll never forget. It was the first time I ever heard anyone say this, although I've heard it several times since. I was asking her about how she maintained her faith through the pain, the disappointments, the treatments, and the complexity of living with cancer. She smiled and said, "Once I was able to accept the cancer as coming from the hand of my heavenly Father, I was okay." I was stunned. Cancer, from God? She went on to explain that as a child of God she believed that God had the final say-so over what could and could not enter her life. She didn't pretend that cancer was a good thing. And Debbie didn't view God as the cause of her cancer. But she accepted it as part of his plan for her. She told me, "In the beginning I would argue with God. I told him that I had more to do and that I didn't have time to be sick. But as long as I argued, I had no peace. Once I accepted this as part of his will for me, I was okay." Debbie slipped out of this life into the next with friends holding hands around her bed, singing her favorite worship choruses. Some of Debbie's dreams never came true. But she never doubted God's faithfulness or love for her. Even in the most excruciating circumstances, she was able to receive all that came her way as coming from the hand of her Father in heaven. In her own way, she embraced David's words when he said of God, "Let him do to me whatever seems good to him."

So what do you do when your dream can't come true? When you realize that a destination is out of reach? You can be angry—angry with God, angry with life. You can despair. You can try to make something happen anyway. You can try and live your dream through your kids. I've seen that plenty of times. But at the end of your striving and manipulating, nothing will have changed.

You will be just as far away from whatever it is you desired. But now you will be far from God as well.

Your other option is to do what David did, what Debbie did, what hundreds of thousands of believers through the ages have done. You can drop to your knees and cry out in disappointment to your heavenly Father. You can mourn the loss of your dream, then wipe the tears from your eyes and say to God, "Do to me whatever seems good to you. I still believe. I still trust. And I will continue to follow."

As David wept his way out of Jerusalem, he had no idea that one thousand years later, one of his descendants, Jesus of Nazareth, would fall to his knees not too far from that very spot and express this same sentiment. On the night of his arrest, Jesus knew that his time on this earth was drawing to an end. And he did not like the way it was ending. So he prayed, "Father, if you are willing, take this cup from me" (Luke 22:42). In other words, *If I were writing this script, there wouldn't be an arrest. There would be no flogging. And there would be no cross.* But then Jesus echoed the words of David, "Yet not my will, but yours be done" (v. 42). That's the prayer of the man and woman who are faced with a destination not of their choosing but continue to trust the One who has led them there.

What do you do when you realize a destination is out of reach? That a dream won't come true? You pray, "Not my will, but yours be done." And then you rest in the fact that you have done all you can . . . and all you should.

Epilogue

When I was nineteen years old, I took a semester off of college and accompanied my dad to the Bahamas. He stayed for two weeks; I stayed for a whole month. The majority of my time was spent on Man-O-War Cay, one of the Bahamas' many outer islands. Man-O-War is approximately two miles long and about one mile wide at its widest point. While I was there, I met another nineteen-year-old, Michael Albury, who has become a lifelong friend. We were in each other's weddings. Sandra and I spent a week of our honeymoon with Michael and his wife, Nancy, exploring uninhabited beaches and marshes around Abaco.

Michael and I came from very different worlds that demanded entirely different skill sets. He could sail, repair an outboard engine, navigate by the stars, spearfish, and coax grouper out from underneath a coral head with his hands. He could hold his breath for four or five minutes. He was completely comfortable around anything related to water. I, on the other hand, knew how to swim. And not all that well.

Late one afternoon, about two weeks into our friendship, Michael asked me to go with him to an island several miles away to retrieve a houseboat from a neighboring marina. About halfway there, it occurred to me that he was expecting me to drive one of the boats back to Man-O-War. That was an exciting prospect for a city kid. The trip took about an hour. Getting the houseboat ready to transport took longer than we anticipated. So by the time we were ready to pull out of the harbor, the sun was already going down. That's when Michael informed me that the boat we came over in didn't have any lights. Not only was that going to make our crossing dangerous, it was going to make it impossible for us to keep track of each other in the open water.

Michael decided it would be best for me to drive the house-boat, since it had lights. Then he took an old flashlight and lashed it down on the back of the other boat. This was not a Q-Beam—it was a red plastic flashlight that he found in a drawer in the houseboat. I didn't have a good feeling about this. But I didn't have a good feeling about a lot of things we did, and so far they had all turned out okay. (If I had time, I would tell you the story of how he taught me to scuba dive. Actually, *taught* is a stretch.)

So with the sun sinking fast, we fired up our engines and pulled out of the marina. His last instructions to me were to stay about one hundred yards behind but not to lose sight of the light. The flashlight. The red plastic flashlight with the two D batteries that had been in there for . . . well, we didn't really know how old those batteries were.

Everything was fine for the first thirty minutes or so. I was feeling empowered. After all, I was skipper of a forty-foot houseboat. But when the sun finally set and the silhouette of Michael's boat disappeared on that moonless night, I wasn't feeling so empowered. The good news was we had radios. And the other thing working to my advantage was that there weren't any competing lights. We were the only boats out there. As long as I could see his light, I could follow along.

Now, for the next part of the story, you are going to have to use your imagination. Imagine what it would look like to approach a small island on a dark night in a boat. What do you think I found myself looking at? Thousands of white lights all strung out along the shore. And the closer we got, the harder it was to distinguish Michael's flashlight from the hundreds of house lights, dock lights, streetlights, and harbor lights. At times I would lose him completely. And then I would catch a glimpse of a light that was moving. That was Michael. Then I would lose it again.

As we got closer to the island, I remembered that a low seawall protected the harbor. If I accidentally lined up on someone's front porch light, I was liable to run my boat right up on the rocks. Fortunately, Michael could see me just fine. From time to time he would slow down and try to redirect me via the radio. The closer we got to the harbor entrance, the more nervous I became. I knew if I could locate the harbor light that marked the entrance to the harbor, I would be fine. But of course the harbor light was another white light. And to locate it I would need to be somewhere near that part of the island. Meanwhile, I was keeping my eyes on what I hoped was the dim yellow light coming from Michael's little plastic flashlight.

With the shoreline coming into focus, Michael's voice came crackling over the radio.

"Where are you?" he asked.

"I'm right behind you," I responded. Then—"Well, I'm right behind something," I said, trying to bring some levity into a very tense environment.

"I just entered the harbor," he said.

That was my second clue that whatever it was I was lined up on, it wasn't Michael's boat. Now I was really nervous. I put the engine in neutral and stared as hard as I could along the coastline, looking for some sign of the harbor lights. Down to my right I caught sight of what looked like it might be it. I turned the boat in that direction and crept along as slowly as the engine would allow. Twenty minutes later I had the marina in sight. As I was attempting to dock the boat, Michael said, "You had me worried. When I turned around and didn't see you, I thought I was going to have to turn around and come looking." We both laughed, tied up the boats, and chalked it up to another averted disaster.

Truth is, if I had continued in the direction I was headed before Michael's final call, I would have run somebody's houseboat aground. Or worse, I could have sliced open the bottom on a coral head and sunk the thing. Should I have been so lucky as to make it ashore, my good intentions would have counted for nothing.

And my intentions *were* good. Heck, I was doing somebody a

favor. But my direction was off. And in the end, that's what deter-mined the outcome of my journey.

Looking back, the thing that made our crossing so harrowing was not the distance, the weather, or even my inexperience. It was the competing lights. If we had made the trip in the daylight, there wouldn't even be a story to tell. But trying to keep my eye on one light among so many made it one of the most stressful—not to mention dangerous—experiences of my life.

We live in a world full of competing lights. One reason so many people charge into adulthood with such clarity but end up beached far from their desired destination is that they become distracted by all the competing lights. They line up on the wrong beacon. The course you have set relationally, financially, spiritu-ally, and professionally will determine where you end up in each of those respective arenas. This is true regardless of your goals, your dreams, your wishes, or wants. As we've stated repeatedly, the principle of the path trumps all of those things. Your current direction will determine your destination.

As a result of our time together, I hope you have a better idea of how to get from where you are to where you want to be. But the challenge, of course, is that as soon as this chapter ends and the book is closed, everything in your world will be exactly as you left it. *Knowing* doesn't make the difference. *Doing* does. The deci-sions you make will determine the direction and the destination of your life. Choose wisely.

Study Guide

This discussion guide is designed to help you grasp the key concepts found in *The Principle of the Path*. For each chapter in the book, you will find a corresponding discussion section with several features: a "Key Idea" entry summarizes the primary point of each chapter; "Key Truths" asks you to react to some of the main ideas developed in each chapter; "Key Questions" asks you to ponder and apply the core ideas of each chapter; and "Key Wisdom" invites you to consider some relevant Bible passages that undergird the ideas in each chapter. The discussion guide is suitable for either group study or individual reflection.

1

SWAMP MY RIDE

Key Idea: Embracing the principle of the path will empower you to identify the paths that lead to the destinations you desire, while avoiding regret.

Key Truths:

1. You can leverage the principle of the path for your benefit or ignore it and reap a harvest of regret.

   • How can you begin leveraging this principle for your benefit?

   • Why does ignoring the principle of the path lead to a harvest of regret?

   • How are you currently leveraging the principle of the path? Explain.

2. The principle of the path impacts your life every day.

   • How has it impacted your life so far?

   • How is this principle impacting your life today?

3. The principle of the path follows you. It's not a law. You can break a law. But the principle of the path has the power to break you.

   • How does this principle "follow" you?

   • How can this principle "break" you?

Key Questions:

1. Describe how the principle of the path is currently affecting each of the following areas of your life:

   - Marriage
   - Family
   - Job
   - Finance
   - Church
   - Physical health

2. Describe a time when you thought you were taking a shortcut in life, only to discover that it led to a dead end.

Key Wisdom:

1. Read Psalm 16:11.

   - What "path" is mentioned here?
   - To what destination does this path lead?

2. Read Psalm 119:105.

   - How does the Bible illuminate your life path?
   - How does your current use of the Bible make it a "lamp" for your feet?

2

WHY BAD THINGS HAPPEN TO SMART PEOPLE

Key Idea: Direction—not intention—determines your destination.

Key Truths:

1. Recognizing the distinction between a *solution* and a *path* is the first step in understanding the principle of the path.

   - What is the difference between a "solution" and a "path"?

   - Why does understanding this distinction help you understand this principle?

2. Cars have problems that can be fixed. Computers have problems that can be fixed. Lawn mowers have problems that can be fixed. But generally speaking, people have directions that need to be changed.

   - What are the biggest problems in your life right now?

   - How could you diminish or get rid of those problems by changing a life direction?

3. Simply put, you and I will win or lose in life by the paths we choose.

   - Do you think you are winning or losing in life by the paths you have chosen? Explain.

- If you think you may be losing in life, how can you change the paths you have chosen?

Key Questions:

1. Where do you think the path you're currently on will take you? Explain.

2. Describe the destination you wish to reach. Is the path you're on likely to take you there? Explain.

3. Does your intention for your life line up with your current direction? Explain.

Key Wisdom:

1. Read Matthew 7:13.

   - What two roads (or paths) are described here?

   - To what destination do each of these roads lead?

   - On which road do you think you're traveling? Explain.

2. Read 1 Kings 11:1–11.

   - What path did Solomon choose as described here?

   - What had God said about choosing this path?

   - Describe the ramifications of his choice.

   - How do you think such a wise man could make such a foolish choice?

3

THE GREAT DISCONNECT

Key Idea: If you want to move in a certain direction, you have to choose the right path.

Key Truths:

1. It seems that most people have a propensity for choosing paths that do not lead in the direction they want to go.

   • Why do you think people tend to choose paths that lead away from where they want to go?

   • What path have you chosen that led you away from your desired destination?

2. We are quick to ask for forgiveness but slow to actually repent and walk away from our sin.

   • What's the difference between asking for forgiveness and repenting?

   • In what area(s) of life does it seem most difficult for you to truly repent? Explain.

3. Choosing the wrong path in life can cost you precious years.

   • How can (or has) choosing the wrong path cost you years?

- Describe someone you know who has chosen a wrong path that has cost him or her years.

Key Questions:

1. What disconnects exist in your life? Explain.

2. What discrepancies exist between what you desire and what you are doing? Explain.

3. Are your intentions in alignment with your direction? Explain.

Key Wisdom:

1. Read Proverbs 7:6–27.

   - What path did the young man described here take? (v. 8)
   - Why does claiming some sort of connection to God not guarantee that you'll choose the right path? (v. 14)
   - What role can marketing play in choosing a deadly path? (v. 21)
   - To what destination does this path lead? (v. 27)

2. Read Jeremiah 6:16.

   - What "paths" does the prophet urge his people to seek out?
   - What results from choosing these designated paths?

4

SHOULD'VE SEEN THAT COMING

Key Idea: The prudent react to what they see on the horizon.

Key Truths:

1. Instead of carefully analyzing the destinations associated with the various path options offered, we tend to charge down the path of least resistance.

   • Why do many believers tend to charge down the path of least resistance?

   • How can you tell ahead of time if a particular path will lead you to a destination you desire? What process do you use?

2. The prudent act as if *then* is *now*; as if the *future* is the *present.* The simple respond as if tomorrow will always be tomorrow.

   • What does it mean to *act* is if the future is the present?

   • What is so dangerous about acting as if tomorrow will never come?

3. For some behaviors there is a point of no return. There is a point at which it becomes impossible to sidestep consequences.

- Is it possible to determine when one reaches a "point of no return"? Explain.

- Describe a time when it became impossible for you to sidestep consequences.

4. Being forgiven does not override experiencing consequences.

   - What is the difference between being forgiven and experiencing consequences?

   - Why does forgiveness not override consequences?

5. In an effort to be wise, you may appear to be foolish, even fearful. You look a bit silly *now* because you are taking steps to avoid something bad *later*.

   - How can wisdom sometimes appear to be foolish or fearful?

   - How can you resist the urge to give in to charges of appearing foolish or fearful?

Key Questions:

1. If you could go back in time, what would you tell yourself at seventeen—and what difference might it have made if you had actually taken your own advice?

2. How can you see trouble coming long before it arrives?

3. How can you acquire the wisdom to know what you should do to handle some future trouble?

Key Wisdom:

1. Read Proverbs 27:12.

   • How does this verse describe a "prudent" man? What sort of action does he take?

   • How does this verse describe a "simple" man? How is his destiny different from that of the wise man? What makes the difference?

2. Read Psalm 73:1–20.

   • What big mistake did the psalmist say he made?

   • How are we often tempted to make the same mistake?

   • What was the cure for this mistake? (vv. 17–20)

5

THE HEART OF THE MATTER

Key Idea: To find the path that will take you where you want to go, you must break the cycle of self-deception.

Key Truths:

1. Our problem stems from the fact that we are not on a *truth quest.*

   • What is meant by a "truth quest"?

   • Are you on such a quest? Why or why not?

2. When the promise of happiness points in one direction while wisdom, truth, integrity, and common sense point in another, that's when really smart people start doing really stupid things.

   • How would you describe "happiness"? How strongly does your pursuit of it influence your decisions?

   • Describe some smart people you know who did stupid things when they allowed their pursuit of happiness to cloud their better judgment.

3. We have a hard time leveling with ourselves. We deceive ourselves about why we choose the things we choose. And then we spin a web of excuses to protect ourselves, excuses that over time we come to believe.

   • Do you have a hard time leveling with yourself? Explain.

   • How have you deceived yourself about why you have made some of your own choices?

   • Describe an excuse you have given that you came to believe over time.

4. When you are willing to come clean with yourself about the uncomfortable truth behind your choices, you're on the verge of freedom.

   • Analyze three of your biggest choices made within the last month. What motivated each of those choices?

- How does "coming clean" with yourself about the truth behind your choices put you on the verge of freedom? Freedom from what?

Key Questions:

1. Can you think of a time when you lied to yourself in order to make a bad decision seem more acceptable? If so, describe what happened.

2. Have you ever sold yourself on what you *wanted* to do rather than what you *ought* to have done? If so, explain.

3. Why is it that our problems rarely stem from a lack of information or insight?

4. In what way is a lack of honesty the real problem?

5. How would you answer each of the following questions about an option you are currently contemplating?
   - Why am I doing this, really?
   - If someone in my circumstances came to me for advice, what course of action would I recommend?
   - In light of my past experience, my future hopes, and my dreams, what is the wise thing to do?

Key Wisdom:

1. Read Jeremiah 17:9–10.

   • How does God describe the human heart? How does this truth complicate things for us?

   • How does God respond to this truth? How does this revelation make you feel? Explain.

2. Read John 8:32.

   • What kind of "truth" is Jesus talking about in this verse?

   • What will knowing this truth do for you?

6

My Italian Job

Key Idea: Choosing the right path begins with *submitting* to the One who knows what's best for you better than *you* know what's best for you.

Key Truths:

1. Your failure to trust or submit to our heavenly Father can lead you to unintended and undesirable destinations.

   • What does it mean to "trust" or "submit to" your heavenly Father? What does such trust or submission look like?

- How can a failure to trust God waste years? Describe a situation in which you saw this take place.

2. Choosing the right path begins with *submission*, not information.

   - In what way does submission differ from information in this context?

   - How have you sometimes confused submission with information?

3. Submission—not talent, information, or insight—is the key to good decisions.

   - Why is submission more important than talent, information, or insight in making good decisions?

   - In what areas of life do you find it easiest to submit to God? In what areas of life do you find it most difficult?

Key Questions:

1. Do you normally surrender to the will of your heavenly Father, or do you tend to lean on your own wisdom and insight? Explain.

2. Do you acknowledge God in all your ways, or do you tend to pick and choose? Explain.

3. What makes you hesitate to give God full access to every part of your life?

4. What do you fear will happen if you fully submit to God?

Key Wisdom:

1. Read 1 Kings 3:7–13.

   • How did Solomon's prayer demonstrate his submission to God?

   • How did God respond to Solomon's request?

2. Read Proverbs 3:5–6.

   • How do you trust in the Lord "with all your heart"?

   • What does it mean to "acknowledge" God in all your ways?

   • What promise does God give to those who follow this instruction?

7

THE STORY YOU WILL TELL

Key Idea: One never accomplishes the will of God by breaking the law of God, violating the principles of God, or ignoring the wisdom of God.

Key Truths:

1. Your decision-making environments are not emotionally neutral.

   • Why are decision-making environments never emotionally neutral?

   • How could recognizing this change the way you make decisions?

2. Emotionally charged decision-making environments make it almost impossible to gain the perspective you need to choose paths that take you where you want to go.

   • Describe an emotionally charged decision-making environment that you recently faced.

   • How does your perspective change in the midst of an emotionally charged decision-making environment?

3. The law, principles, and wisdom of God provided David with the clarity he needed to do the right thing in the right way at the right time, despite incredible pressure to do otherwise.

   • How did the law give David the clarity he needed?

   • How did the principles of the Bible give David the clarity he needed?

   • How did the wisdom of God give David the clarity he needed?

- Describe a time when incredible pressure changed a decision you had to make.

Key Questions:

1. Does some option you're currently considering violate God's law? Has God already spoken on this matter? If so, how?

2. Does some option you're currently considering violate a principle? If so, how?

3. What outcome are you expecting from a decision you're about to make? Does the option you're considering naturally lead to that outcome? If so, how?

4. In light of the story you want to tell, what is the wise thing to do? Explain.

Key Wisdom:

1. Read 1 Samuel 24:4–7.
   - How did the law of God argue against taking Saul's life?
   - How did the principles of God argue against taking Saul's life?
   - How did the wisdom of God argue against taking Saul's life?

- Why was sparing Saul's life the wise thing to do? In what way did it appear unwise? What pressure did David have to overcome? Why would this have been difficult to accomplish?

2. Read 1 Samuel 3:3–23.

- What command did God give to Saul? How did Saul respond to this command?
- How did Saul disobey the command of God?
- How did Saul defy the principles of God?
- How did Saul ignore the wisdom of God?
- What was the result?

8

A LITTLE HELP FROM OUR FRIENDS

Key Idea: You will never reach your full potential without tapping into the wisdom of others.

Key Truths:

1. The herd assumption is when you *assume* that since everybody you know is doing something the same way, it must be all right.

- Why is it so easy to fall into line with the herd assumption?

- How can you protect yourself from falling into line with the herd assumption?

2. It is always wise to learn what we can from people whose lives and lifestyles reflect our own goals and aspirations.

   - What goals and aspirations do you have? Who do you know who already reflects these goals and aspirations?

   - Identify someone from whom you'd like to learn how he or she achieved some worthwhile goal. What keeps you from asking this person about his or her experience?

3. Successful people know what they don't know and they are quick to go to people who do know.

   - In what key area(s) of life do you lack the knowledge you need to succeed?

   - Who do you know who has this knowledge?

4. Pray for wisdom, and then seek outside assistance.

   - Why does seeking human counsel not contradict seeking God's wisdom through prayer?

   - In what area of your life do you most need wisdom? Are you praying for it? Are you seeking outside counsel for it? Explain.

5. No one gets to the place where he or she no longer needs wise counsel.

- Do you agree with this statement? Why or why not?
- Describe the wisest counselor you know. What makes this person so wise?

Key Questions:

1. Did you consciously choose your life maps? Did you inherit them? Did you pick up a set of maps as a reaction to the way you were raised?

2. Do you seek advice from those who are older and wiser? Explain.

3. Whose pattern are you following? Whose journey are you emulating? Why?

4. How can you gain a better understanding of how a successful person came to have a great marriage, family, and financial situation?

Key Wisdom:

Solomon had more to say about seeking the wisdom and direction of others than any other biblical author. What did he say about this practice in each of the following verses?

Proverbs 1:5; 11:14; 12:15; 13:10; 15:22; 19:20

9

ATTENTION RETENTION

Key Idea: What gets our attention determines our direction and, ultimately, our destination.

Key Truths:

1. The things that tend to grab or capture your attention are often things you should avoid.

   • What negative things tend to grab your attention?

   • In what way(s) are these things undesirable?

2. Whereas *emotion* fuels the things that grab your attention, *intentionality* fuels your decision to give certain things your attention.

   • How would you define *intentionality*?

   • How can you train yourself to allow intentionality to override emotion?

3. A sense of loss keeps you from paying attention to the things that deserve your attention and would serve you best in the future.

   • How does a sense of loss keep you from paying attention to the things that really deserve your attention?

   • Name several good ways to keep such a sense of loss from diverting your attention.

4. Over and over, God reminds you that the things to which you harness your attention direct your life.

- To what things have you harnessed your attention?
- How have these things directed your life? Are you satisfied with this? Explain.

Key Questions:

1. What or who has your attention now? Is this a good thing? Explain.

2. Has anything or anyone captured your attention in a way that distracts you from the things or people that deserve your attention? Explain.

3. Are you giving an inordinate amount of attention to something that a year ago wasn't even on your radar screen? If so, what is it?

4. Is there anyone or anything you are giving attention to that, if it were to become public, would be embarrassing . . . or worse? Explain.

5. What are you putting off?

6. Does your spouse or someome close to you keep bringing up the same stuff over and over? If so, what?

7. Have you heard yourself getting defensive over things that you swear are "really no big deal"? If so, what?

Key Wisdom:

1. Read Proverbs 4:25–27.

   • What does the author instruct us to do with our eyes?

   • What does the author instruct us to do with our feet?

   • What is the author trying to help his reader do? (v. 27)

2. Read Matthew 14:24–31.

   • On what did Peter *first* fix his eyes? What was the result?

   • On what did Peter *ultimately* fix his eyes? What was the result?

   • If Jesus had not intervened, what would have been Peter's destination?

10

ROAD CLOSED

Key Idea: When it dawns on you that your dreams can't come true, the best response is to lean hard on the One who allowed your disappointment to occur.

Key Truths:

1. At some point we all wake to the realization that *it*— whatever *it* is—is not going to happen for us.

    • Describe a time when "it" didn't happen for you.

    • How did you respond to this outcome?

2. God can be trusted but not manipulated.

    • Can you think of a time when you experienced God's faithfulness?

    • How have you found God to be incapable of being manipulated?

3. The only option other than submitting to God is to run from the only One who can bring comfort when you need comfort the most.

    • Why is running from God the only option other than submitting to him?

    • Why do we run from God when he is the only One who can bring us comfort?

4. When you realize that a destination is out of reach, you can be angry, you can despair, you can try to make something happen anyway, you can try and live your dream through your kids—but at the end of your striving and manipulating, nothing will have changed.

- When you realize a destination is out of reach, how do you normally respond?

- Describe a time when you felt far from God. What led you to that place?

Key Questions:

1. What do you normally do when factors outside your control make it impossible to get from where you are to where you want to be?

2. When a dream evaporates, what is hard about saying to God, "Do to me whatever seems good to you. I still believe. I still trust. And I will continue to follow"?

3. How does praying, "Not my will, but yours be done," help you to rest in the fact that you have done all you can and all you should?

Key Wisdom:

1. Read 2 Samuel 7:1–7.

- What "destination" did David have in his heart?

- What made it impossible for him to reach this destination?

- How did he respond?

2. Read Luke 22:42.

- What "destination" did Jesus want to avoid?

- What was more important to Jesus than his desired destination?

- How can he be our chief example when we realize what we want will not happen?